INDONESIA
in Pictures

Jeffrey Zuehlke

Twenty-First Century Books

Contents

Lerner Publishing Group realizes that current information and statistics quickly become out of date. To extend the usefulness of the Visual Geography Series, we developed www.vgsbooks.com, a website offering links to up-to-date information, as well as in-depth material, on a wide variety of subjects. All of the websites listed on www.vgsbooks.com have been carefully selected by researchers at Lerner Publishing Group. However, Lerner Publishing Group is not responsible for the accuracy or suitability of the material on any website other than www.lernerbooks.com. It is recommended that students using the Internet be supervised by a parent or teacher. Links on www.vgsbooks.com will be regularly reviewed and updated as needed.

► Topography. Greater Sunda Islands. The Lesser Sunda Islands and the Malukus. Papua. Rivers. Climate. Natural Resources and Environmental Concerns. Fauna and Flora. Cities.

► Early History. Srivijaya and Javanese Kingdoms. Majapahit Kingdom. Europeans Arrive. The Second Mataram Kingdom and Shifts in European Control. The Java War and Dutch Administration. Political Parties Form. World War II and Postwar Developments. Sukarno and Suharto. End of the Suharto Era and the Beginning of Democracy. Government.

► Ethnic Groups and Language. Education. Health.

Website address: www.lernerbooks.com

Twenty-First Century Books
A division of Lerner Publishing Group
241 First Avenue North
Minneapolis, MN 55401 U.S.A.

web enhanced @ www.vgsbooks.com

CULTURAL LIFE 44

▶ Religion. Folk Arts and Crafts. Holidays and Festivals. Food. Literature and Media. Sports and Recreation.

THE ECONOMY 56

▶ Industry, Mining, and Energy. Services, Tourism, and Trade. Agriculture, Forestry, and Fishing. Transportation and Communications. The Future.

FOR MORE INFORMATION

Library of Congress Cataloging-in-Publication Data

Zuehlke, Jeffrey, 1968–
     Indonesia in pictures / by Jeffrey Zuehlke.—Rev. & expanded.
         p.   cm. – (Visual geography series)
     Includes bibliographical references and index.
     ISBN-13: 978-0-8225-2074-0 (lib. bdg. : alk. paper)
     ISBN-10: 0-8225-2074-5 (lib. bdg. : alk. paper)
     1. Indonesia—Juvenile literature. 2. Indonesia—Pictorial works—Juvenile literature. I. Title. II. Visual
geography series
DS615.Z84 2006
959.8—dc22   2005002893

Manufactured in the United States of America
1 2 3 4 5 6 – BP – 11 10 09 08 07 06

INTRODUCTION

On December 26, 2004, a tremendous earthquake, registering a magnitude of 9.0 on the Richter scale, occurred on the ocean floor off the west coast of the Indonesian island of Sumatra. The violent tremors created a massive tsunami (tidal wave) that struck not only the Sumatran coast but also the shores of Thailand, Burma, India, Sri Lanka, Bangladesh, and several Indian Ocean island chains, as well as the east coast of Africa. Due to its close proximity to the earthquake's epicenter, Sumatra was by far the hardest hit. Entire towns and villages were smashed to pieces and washed out to sea by the huge walls of water.

The world reacted with horror as news of the disaster spread. In the following days, the sheer scale of the devastation unfolded and the death toll skyrocketed to more than 200,000 people. Meanwhile, relief efforts, led by the United Nations (or UN, a global humanitarian and peacekeeping organization) and the armed forces of the United States and Australia, rushed to the scene to provide clean drinking water,

food, and medicine to the survivors. Governments and private citizens from around the world responded to the tragedy by contributing billions of dollars in aid to help the victims.

The Indonesian Ministry of Health estimates that the tsunami killed 122,232 Indonesians. Yet the true death toll is probably much higher, as 114,000 Indonesians are still missing and unaccounted for.

Most of the damage to Indonesia occurred in the province of Aceh, a chiefly Muslim region that has been plagued by political violence for many years. Members of the Free Aceh Movement (known by its Indonesian acronym, GAM) have fought for independence from Indonesia since the 1970s. The Indonesian government responded to this separatist movement by sending in troops to crush the rebels.

Natural disasters and separatist strife are not new to Indonesia. In fact, the most powerful volcanic eruption in recorded history—the Krakatau eruption—occurred in Indonesia in 1883. Meanwhile, the country's thousands of islands are home to hundreds of ethnic groups,

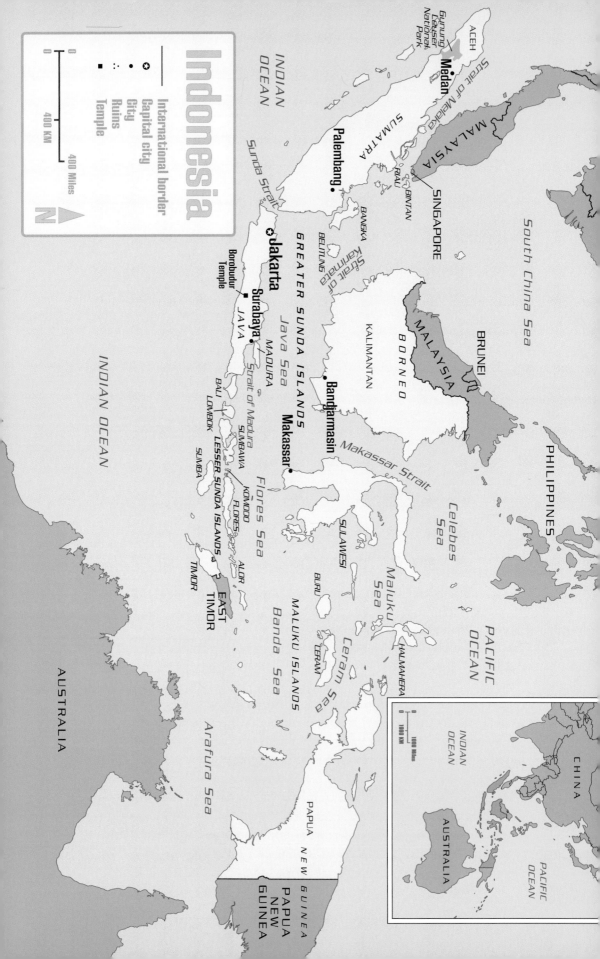

many of whom desire self-rule, and conflicts between separatists and the government have been fought off and on—most notably in East Timor and Papua—for many years.

These conflicts have caused some observers to question the long-term future of Indonesia as a nation. And in fact, few Indonesians would have seen themselves as part of a single nation prior to the twentieth century. The Indonesia of modern times is largely a creation of the Dutch, who ruled much of the archipelago (group of islands) beginning in the early 1600s. But even before the country gained its independence from Dutch colonial rule in 1949, Indonesia's future leaders were working hard to forge Indonesia's identity as a single political unit. The country's motto is Unity in Diversity, and the country's political philosophy, Pancasila, emphasizes unity between the nation's hundreds of ethnic groups.

This very diversity makes Indonesia a fascinating place. From the packed and bustling streets of the capital, Jakarta, to the dense and sparsely populated forests of Papua, the country is home to a mind-boggling mix of peoples, cultures, and lifestyles. Although the vast majority of Indonesians are Muslims (Indonesia is the world's largest Muslim nation in terms of population), the nation's many different ethnic groups have each developed their own unique ways of following the Muslim faith. Many Indonesians blend Islam with their traditional beliefs and even with other religions such as Buddhism and Hinduism.

The name *Indonesia* was coined by a British geographer, James Richardson Logan, to describe the vast archipelago of islands lying off the Indian subcontinent. The word basically means "Indian Islands," as the word *Indo* comes from "Indian" and *nesia* comes from "nesos," the Greek word for "islands." The British also used the term Further India to describe the archipelago.

The unique melting pot of beliefs and cultures that makes up Indonesia owes much to the influence of outsiders. Occupying the sea-lanes that separate the Pacific and Indian oceans, the archipelago has been a rest-and-resupply stop for traders and travelers for centuries. In modern times, a large percentage of the world's trade still passes through Indonesia's waters. With its rich and colorful cultures, wondrous natural beauty, and key strategic location, Indonesia is a source of endless fascination to visitors and scholars alike.

THE LAND

The Republic of Indonesia occupies most of the largest island groups in the world—the Malay Archipelago. This group of islands also includes the Philippines and other territories that are part of Malaysia and Australia. The Malay Archipelago is south of the Southeast Asian mainland and divides the Indian Ocean from the Pacific Ocean. Indonesia itself consists of an estimated 17,508 islands, of which about 6,000 are inhabited. The republic covers 705,192 square miles (1,826,440 square kilometers) in land area, which is an area equal in size to about one-fifth of the United States.

Indonesia stretches over 3,200 miles (5,150 km) in an arc that begins west of the Malay Peninsula and continues south and east to New Guinea. The nation has land boundaries with Malaysia and Brunei on the island of Borneo, with Papua New Guinea on the island of New Guinea, and with the newly independent East Timor on the island of Timor. Touching its territory are many bodies of water, including the Java, Flores, Banda, Maluku, and Ceram seas.

The islands of Indonesia can be classified into four main groups. The Greater Sunda Islands consist of the archipelago's four largest land-masses—Java, Sulawesi, Sumatra, and Kalimantan (the Indonesian part of Borneo). A smaller chain—the Lesser Sunda Islands—is made up of Bali, Lombok, Sumbawa, Flores, Sumba, Alor, and Timor.

The third group is the Maluku Islands (often called the Spice Islands). They include Halmahera, Ceram, Buru, and many other smaller islands. Papua (known as Irian Jaya from the 1970s until 2000) is the Indonesian half of New Guinea and forms the fourth topographical group.

Topography

Many geologists think that in prehistoric times, Indonesia's western islands were part of the Asian continent and the eastern territories were connected to Australia. Over time the earth's landmasses slowly shifted. The ocean level rose when the last major Ice Age ended about twelve thousand years ago. Water covered all but the highest portions of a long mountain range that forms the Indonesian archipelago.

Indonesian territory consists of lowlands, high plains, and mountains. Lowlands stretch through river valleys along the coasts of the major islands. Plateaus that connect mountainous areas form many of the high plains. Mountains and volcanoes are the main feature of most of Indonesia's islands.

Indonesia is in the so-called Ring of Fire—a zone of frequent earthquakes and volcanic activity that includes the east coasts of Asia and Australia and the west coast of North America.

A Central Mountain range extends the length of the Indonesian archipelago. The highest mountain—Puncak Jaya in Papua—rises to 16,535 feet (5,040 meters) above sea level. The country contains more than four hundred volcanoes, sixty of which are active. Bali's most famous volcano, Gunung Agung, last erupted in 1963 and killed nearly two thousand people. The nation's most spectacular volcano is Anak Krakatau. It forms a small island in the Sunda Strait between Java and Sumatra. In 1883 this island volcano (then known as Krakatau) erupted with such force that debris from the explosion landed as far away as Madagascar, off the eastern coast of Africa. In the decades following Krakatau's blast, a small but growing new volcano has emerged from the sea.

Balinese people consider **Gunung Agung** the navel of the world and celebrate the volcano as the holiest peak on the island.

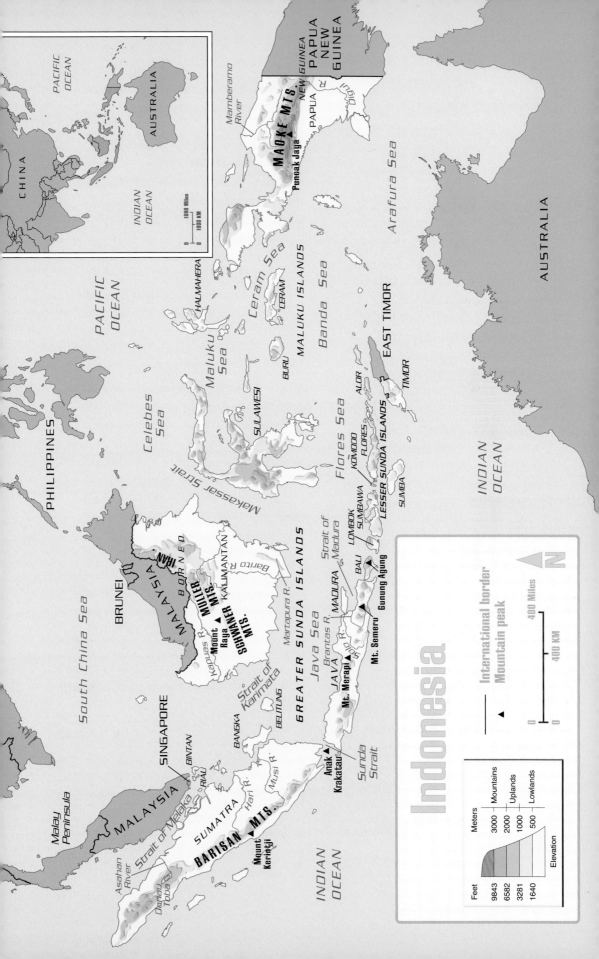

Indonesia

PACIFIC OCEAN

AUSTRALIA

CHINA

INDIAN OCEAN

0   1000 Miles
0   1000 KM

PACIFIC OCEAN

PHILIPPINES

South China Sea

MALAYSIA

BRUNEI

Malay Peninsula

MALAYSIA

SINGAPORE

BINTAN

RIAU

Strait of Malaka

Asahan River

Danau Toba

SUMATRA

BARISAN MTS.

Mount Keringtji

Hari R.

Musi R.

INDIAN OCEAN

BANGKA

BELITUNG

Strait of Karimata

Sunda Strait

Anak Krakatau

Java Sea

GREATER SUNDA ISLANDS

BORNEO

KALIMANTAN

IHAN

MULLER MTS.

Mount Raya

SCHWANER MTS.

Kapuas R.

Barito R.

Martapura R.

Makassar Strait

SULAWESI

Celebes Sea

HALMAHERA

Maluku Sea

Ceram Sea

CERAM

MALUKU ISLANDS

BURU

Banda Sea

JAVA

Mt. Merapi

Brantas R.

Strait of Madura

MADURA

Mt. Semeru

BALI

Gunung Agung

LOMBOK

SUMBAWA

LESSER SUNDA ISLANDS

KOMODO

FLORES

ALOR

SUMBA

Flores Sea

EAST TIMOR

TIMOR

Arafura Sea

INDIAN OCEAN

AUSTRALIA

NEW GUINEA

PAPUA NEW GUINEA

MAOKE MTS.

Puncak Jaya

PAPUA

Mamberamo River

Dig R.

Elevation

Feet	Meters	
9843	3000	Mountains
6582	2000	Uplands
3281	1000	
1640	500	Lowlands

International border

▲ Mountain peak

N

0   400 Miles
0   400 KM

KRAKATAU

In 1883 Indonesia was the site of one of the most powerful volcanic eruptions in recorded history. Beginning on August 26, Krakatau, a volcano in the Sunda Strait between Java and Sumatra, erupted in a series of explosions. The climactic blasts occurred the next day, creating an ash cloud 17 miles (27 km) high and launching about 5 cubic miles (21 cubic km) of rock into the air. The explosions—easily the loudest in recorded history—were heard in Australia, thousands of miles away.

All life on the island was destroyed—buried in ash—and the entire surrounding region was blanketed in darkness for two and one-half days. In the coming months, the massive ash cloud spread, leaving debris over 300,000 square miles (800,000 sq. km). Areas closest to the eruption were buried in as much as 200 feet (61 m) of ash. (In some spots, the ash was so thick that ships could not sail through it.) The thinnest ash particles drifted around the world several times, creating spectacular red sunsets for an entire year. The eruption also triggered a series of tsunamis that struck coastlines as far away as South America and the Hawaiian Islands, killing about 36,000 people.

Indonesians call this volcano Anak Krakatau (child of Krakatau).

▶ Greater Sunda Islands

Sumatra, the Indonesian island closest to the Southeast Asian mainland, is 1,000 miles (1,609 km) long and measures about 250 miles (402 km) across at its widest point. Its eastern half consists of lowland forests and swamps. The Barisan Mountains run almost the entire length of Sumatra. Many of the range's volcanic peaks reach heights between 6,000 and 12,000 feet (1,829 to 3,658 m). The island's tallest summit is Mount Kerintji (12,483 feet/3,805 m). Western Sumatra has a narrow coastal plain, which is most fertile in the north. To the northeast, the Strait of Melaka separates the island from the Malay Peninsula. To the southeast, the Sunda Strait divides Sumatra from the island of Java.

Java—which extends eastward from the southern tip of Sumatra—contains only 7 percent of the country's land area. More than 60 percent of the nation's population, however, reside on Java.

The island is 660 miles (1,062 km) from west to east and about 100 miles (161 km) from north to south. The volcanic mountain chain that begins in Sumatra continues on Java, but the terrain is far less rugged than on other islands. The average height of the Central Mountains is about 8,000 feet (2,438 m). Java's highest peak, Mount Semeru, climbs to just over 12,000 feet (3,658 m). The northern side of the island has wide, fertile plains, and the western region is a large highland plateau. On Java's southern side, the mountains drop sharply into the Indian Ocean.

Most of the large island of Borneo, located north of Java, belongs to Indonesia. Kalimantan, the Indonesian portion of the island, occupies the southern two-thirds of Borneo. Malaysia and Brunei share the remainder of the island.

The Schwaner Mountains lie in the southwestern part of Kalimantan. The tallest peak in this generally low-lying range is Mount Raya, at 7,474 feet (2,278 m). The Muller Mountains run in a north-south direction along the center of the island and average 4,000 to 5,000 feet (1,219 to 1,524 m) in elevation. Along Kalimantan's boundary with Malaysia stretch the Iran Mountains, with peaks that climb to nearly 10,000 feet (3,048 m). The southern coast of the island has large areas of swamp that, along with the upland areas, make roads difficult to build.

Sulawesi (formerly called Celebes) lies east of Kalimantan across the Makassar Strait. Unusually shaped, this island has four peninsulas that extend from a central landmass. Sulawesi is mostly mountainous, but its narrow coastal plains are suitable for farming.

The Lesser Sunda Islands and the Malukus

The most famous of the Lesser Sunda Islands is Bali. Lying just over 1 mile (1.6 km) east of Java, Bali has a wide central plain. Gunung Agung (10,308 feet/3,142 m) is the tallest peak in a group of volcanoes in northern Bali. Lombok, Sumbawa, Sumba, Flores, Timor, and smaller nearby islands form the rest of the Lesser Sunda group.

Located east of Sulawesi, the Malukus include about one thousand pieces of territory. The largest are Halmahera, Ceram, and Buru. Known as the Spice Islands to sixteenth-century European explorers, these islands are mountainous, and many are of volcanic origin. Surrounding coral reefs hamper navigation in this region.

Papua

New Guinea—the world's largest island after Greenland—lies east of the Malukus. The Indonesian territory of Papua is in the western half of New Guinea and shares the island with the country of Papua New Guinea. Rain forests cover more than 80 percent of Papua. The Maoke Mountains—the tallest range in Indonesia—run in a west-east direction through the state. Several peaks reach 16,000 feet (4,877 m) and are covered with snow year-round.

Papua's northern coastal plain is narrow, and its southern coast is wide and swampy. Because most of the land is unsuitable for farming, Papua is the least populated of the major Indonesian regions.

Rivers

Indonesia's rivers are major travel routes on many of the islands. In some places, waterways provide the only transportation links between settlements. All the rivers on Sumatra begin in the Barisan Mountains. The rivers that flow to the east—such as the 450-mile-long (724 km) Hari and the 325-mile-long (523 km) Musi—are longer than those that run westward into the Indian Ocean. The Asahan River in northern Sumatra is the outlet for Lake Toba, a large body of water within the Barisan Mountains.

Java's many rivers are short, with the Solo River having the longest course at just over 300 miles (483 km). The Brantas River in central Java travels north for 195 miles (314 km) and passes the city of Surabaya before it empties into the Strait of Madura.

Waterways also crisscross Kalimantan and Papua. In western Kalimantan, the Kapuas River flows west into the Strait of Karimata, and the Barito River goes south into the Java Sea. The Mamberamo River—Papua's longest waterway—runs northward for 500 miles (805 km) from the Maoke Mountains to the Pacific Ocean. The island's 400-mile-long (644 km) Digul River travels south from the mountains into the Arafura Sea.

Indonesia's rivers have great potential for generating electricity. The government has built a number of hydropower plants on Java, where rivers supply some of the electricity for the heavily populated island.

Climate

Located on the equator, Indonesia has a tropical climate. Although overall temperatures normally range between 66° and 96°F (19 to 36°C), the average temperature at sea level is 79°F (24°C). Temperatures in the mountains are cooler than temperatures in the lowlands.

Because of the country's location on the equator, days and nights are nearly the same length in Indonesia. Only a forty-eight-minute difference exists between the longest and the shortest days of the year. Morning and evening twilight times are extremely short, since the sun rises and sets abruptly.

Monsoons—seasonal winds that bring either moist or dry air to the country—largely determine weather conditions in the archipelago. Although rainfall is abundant year-round, a wet season occurs from November to April, when the rain-filled northeast monsoon arrives from the Indian Ocean. In May a dry season begins when the southwest monsoon, as well as dry air from Australia, blows until October.

Even during the dry season, humidity is almost always high in Indonesia, and the heaviest rains fall in the mountains, with levels averaging 240 inches (610 centimeters) each year in some regions. Annual rainfall is usually 80 inches (203 cm) in Jakarta, and Sumatra and Kalimantan receive between 120 and 144 inches (305 to 366 cm). Some small islands, such as Komodo in the Lesser Sunda chain, are extremely dry.

Natural Resources and Environmental Concerns

Indonesia possesses a wide variety of natural resources, and oil is its most valuable mineral. Several oil fields on Sumatra have been tapped since the late nineteenth century. In addition to facilities on Sumatra, Java, and other islands, Indonesia operates offshore oil wells in the South China and Java seas. Natural gas is the country's other principal mineral product. Much of the gas is turned into a liquid and sold abroad. Many of the major islands also contain deposits of coal. Profits from the sale of these fuels have funded the nation's economic development.

Tin, nickel, copper, silver, gold, and bauxite (the source of aluminum) are mined on some islands. With its many powerful rivers, the nation has tremendous potential for creating hydroelectric power. However, with the exception of some hydroelectric plants in Java and a plant in Papua, the country has yet to tap much of this renewable energy source. The government has also begun to tap geothermal heat (heat from the earth's interior) as a source of energy.

Indonesia also has abundant forests. In fact, the country is home to 10 percent of the world's forest cover, including the largest rain forest area in Asia and the third-largest rain forest in the world.

Indonesia's forests, however, are under threat. Destructive logging is clearing away trees at an unsustainable rate, and the government has provided logging companies with little incentive to use responsible practices. In fact, in recent years, a large amount of illegal logging has taken place in Indonesia, but the government has so far lacked the resources to enforce the country's logging laws. As a result, environmentally harmful logging has led to serious problems with soil erosion (the deep roots of trees

Indonesia's forests are not only valuable for their wood products. They also act as carbon sinks—areas that convert carbon dioxide into oxygen, helping to offset the effects of global warming.

These women are sitting on recently felled logs after **slash-and-burn** techniques were used to clear this forest in Sumatra.

help to stabilize soil, stopping erosion) that have led to floods and landslides. One landslide in 2003 caused the death of 150 Indonesians.

Misuse of the country's forests has also added to the country's serious air pollution problem. To clear the forests for cropland, many farmers use slash-and-burn techniques. In several cases, human-created forest fires have raged out of control. In one of the worst such episodes, in 1997 and 1998, forest fires consumed nearly 25 million acres (10 million hectares) of Indonesian forest. The fires created so much smoke that much of the country, as well as parts of neighboring Malaysia and Singapore, were shrouded in a dirty haze for months.

Indonesia's air pollution challenges also stem from the country's rapid increase in automobile use. Between 1995 and 2001, the number of motor vehicles in Indonesia nearly doubled, from 12 million to 21 million. This number continues to grow, and air quality issues are made worse by the fact that most Indonesian cars run on leaded gasoline, as opposed to the cleaner unleaded gasoline used in the West. The Indonesian government has instituted a ban on leaded gasoline, but has so far struggled to enforce it due to a lack of financial resources.

The country also faces challenges with its water supply. Indonesia's cities lack proper sewage systems. For example, a recent report noted that less than 3 percent of the population of Jakarta is connected to a sewerage system. The rest of the population use less effective septic tank systems or dispose of waste directly into rivers and canals. As a result, an estimated 90 percent of Jakarta's water wells are contaminated. These problems are compounded because industrial water pollution is largely unregulated by the government.

The Indonesian government has acknowledged these environmental problems. Several programs aimed at cleaning up the country's air and water and to conserve its forests and natural habitats were designed and implemented in the early 1990s. Some progress was made during the 1990s, but much of it stalled when Indonesia was struck by the Asian Financial Crisis of 1997. Seeking to recover quickly from the financial devastation of the crisis, the government abandoned many environmentally conscious programs for the sake of productivity or did not enforce laws due to lack of funds. In the early 2000s, most of the laws have yet to be fully brought back into force.

▷ Fauna and Flora

Mismanagement of Indonesia's environment has also harmed the country's wild animal habitats, and Indonesia holds the distinction of having the highest number of endangered species in the world. Endangered Indonesian animals include the orangutan, two species of rhinoceros, the Sumatran elephant, and the Sumatran tiger.

However, despite these challenges, the country is still home to a large and varied mix of animals. For example, many wild boar and crocodiles populate Indonesia. The *kantjil* (mouse deer) plays a role in Indonesian fairy tales similar to that of the clever fox in Western folklore. The water buffalo is the primary work animal on farms.

The Malukus support a great variety of parrots, and Papua is famous for birds of paradise, which have long, brightly colored feathers. Other Indonesian birds include cockatoos, ducks, kingfishers, pheasants, pigeons, and cassowaries. Tuna, scad, mollusks, mackerel, and sharks represent some of the region's marine life.

An **orangutan** mother and her baby relax in a tree in Gunung Leuser National Park in Sumatra. Some of the rarest tropical birds in the world, such as the **bird of paradise,** can be found on Papua.

The island of Komodo is famous for the monitor lizard—often called the Komodo dragon—the world's largest lizard. This creature, which can grow to 10 feet long (3 m), stalks rodents through dry grasslands.

Indonesia's rich soil, tropical climate, and plentiful rainfall provide an ideal environment for a wide variety of plants. The rafflesia, a rain forest plant, uses its roots to attach itself to shrubs and vines. The plant produces a single, giant flower that can grow up to 36 inches (91 cm) wide. When the bloom appears, all other external parts of the rafflesia wither away. One of the best-known flowering trees in Indonesia is the

A rafflesia flower

frangipani. It flourishes mainly in Bali. The large blossoms of this small tree are widely used for temple decorations.

Indonesia grows most of its own fruits, including bananas, breadfruit, guavas, mangoes, papayas, pineapples, and tamarinds. Many edible fruits grow wild, and most of them—such as the small, yellow blimbing and the thorny, green durian—are unfamiliar to westerners.

Indonesia's forests contain many kinds of trees, including camphor, sandalwood, oak, chestnut, fig, banyan, and evergreen. The coastal areas contain mangroves and nipa palms, while tropical rain forests predominate in the interior lowlands. The most commercially important trees on the islands are coconut and rubber trees.

⊙ Cities

About 43 percent of Indonesia's population live in urban centers. The island of Java has several cities with more than a million inhabitants. With 9.3 million residents, the capital, Jakarta, is the nation's largest city. Located at the western end of Java, Jakarta's site has been inhabited for more than one thousand years.

Jakarta contains both seventeenth-century European dwellings and new office buildings. Neighborhoods of modern residential homes contrast with large areas of makeshift housing that have inadequate sanitation services. Jakarta's downtown streets are lined with department stores, marketplaces, open-air shops, and old and new hotels. City officials are working to overcome Jakarta's serious problems, such as traffic congestion and air pollution.

Surabaya is Indonesia's second-largest city. Located on the eastern end of Java, Surabaya has a population of more than 2.5 million people. A trading hub since the fourteenth century, the city is a modern shipping and industrial center.

Traffic sails past glass office buildings on Jalan Thamrin, the main thoroughfare in **Jakarta.** Indonesia's capital is one of the most crowded cities in the world.

Sumatra's two largest cities are Medan (population 2.5 million) and Palembang (population 1.5 million). Founded in the late 1800s by an Islamic leader, Medan is home to one of the largest mosques (Islamic houses of prayer) in Indonesia. Palembang lies on the site of the capital of the Srivijaya kingdom, which flourished in the eleventh century, although little evidence of this past remains. Palembang serves as the center of the nation's oil industry.

The city of Makassar (known as Ujung Pandang from the 1970s until 1999) on Sulawesi is home to 1.3 million residents. Makassar was in its earlier history a gathering place for pirates. Since 1900 the city's inhabitants have concentrated on fishing and shipbuilding as their main economic activities. In Kalimantan about 800,000 people live in the city of Bandjarmasin. Located about 20 miles (32 km) from the mouth of the Martapura River, Bandjarmasin receives oil tankers and transport ships that carry the rubber and timber products of Borneo to overseas markets.

 Visit www.vgsbooks.com for links to websites with additional information about the many things to see and do in Indonesia's many cities, as well as links to websites about Indonesia's weather, natural resources, plants and animals, and more.

HISTORY AND GOVERNMENT

In 1891 archaeologists discovered the remains of an early form of human life on the island of Java. Known by its scientific name as *Homo erectus*, this human being is also called Java man. The discovery indicates that ancestors of modern humans lived on Java during an early stage of human evolution. Scientists have found ancient fossils along riverbeds and in volcanic deposits suggesting that Java man lived about 500,000 years ago.

Early History

Little is known of Indonesia's early inhabitants. Evidence from the late Stone Age indicates that in about 2000 B.C., Malay people from the Southeast Asian mainland began migrating to regions as far east as the western Malukus. These Malays used stone tools and had developed techniques for building wooden houses, weaving, making pottery, and growing rice.

A second migration of Malays came to the Indonesian archipelago about 250 B.C. The newcomers, who used bronze tools, spread as far

east as New Guinea. Settling along the islands' coasts, they forced the earlier Malay immigrants to move inland. For the next few centuries, both groups grew, surviving on cultivated rice and native vegetation.

In time, Indonesian territory provided a rest-and-resupply stop for oceangoing traders who sailed the waters between India and China. Merchants from India arrived on the islands around the first or second century A.D. Beginning in the third century, Indonesians exchanged cloves (dried flowers that are used as a spice and to make oil), timber, and camphor (used in medicines) for Chinese and Indian goods.

Indian traders introduced the Hindu and Buddhist religions, and coastal residents borrowed ideas from these faiths, incorporating them into their own long-held beliefs. Soon coastal communities used both Indian philosophies to develop small, highly organized kingdoms. Indonesians also adopted a form of the Indian Sanskrit alphabet, and members of the royal courts read much of India's religious, political, and scientific literature. Throughout this early stage of Indian influence, little conflict existed between followers of Buddhism and supporters of Hinduism.

Srivijaya and Javanese Kingdoms

By the seventh century, two powerful kingdoms had emerged—Mataram, which was based on Java; and Srivijaya, which had its base near the modern-day Sumatran city of Palembang. The Mataram kingdom reached its high point in the eighth and ninth centuries. This era was marked by the construction of the Borobudur, the largest Buddhist building in the world and one of the most famous sites in Indonesia.

Meanwhile, Srivijaya was also thriving, and Buddhist teachers from both China and India contributed to the kingdom's religious life. Palembang became a center of prayer and study for many Buddhists. By the eleventh century, Srivijaya was at the height of its power. The Srivijayans possessed large parts of Sumatra and Java and controlled many of the sea-lanes around the islands, including the Strait of Melaka and the Sunda Strait. Ships carrying goods between India and China stopped in the archipelago to await strong sailing winds or to

Java's **Borobudur Temple,** which was built in the eighth and ninth centuries, is made of more than one million blocks of stone. The temple's 1,460 narrative panels depict Buddha's life.

trade their cargo. Chinese and Indian merchants and the Srivijayans' Malay neighbors knew the kingdom to be a prominent cultural and trading center.

Between the eleventh and thirteenth centuries, however, the Srivijayan kingdom slowly declined because of attacks by other realms in the region. During roughly the same period, Mataram also experienced a decline as it fought off attacks from outside powers and was weakened by internal divisions.

Meanwhile, several other Hindu and Buddhist kingdoms were developing on Java. Elements of Buddhism and Hinduism blended throughout these realms. In the thirteenth century, the Singasari kingdom brought together Hinduism and Buddhism in the united worship of Siva-Buddha, a divine being who represented the central figure from each of the two religions.

As Indonesia developed its own unique blend of Hinduism and Buddhism, another faith—Islam—began to take hold on the archipelago. Muslim traders brought Islam to Indonesia from the Middle East and converted many Indonesians. After Islam took hold in the trading centers of Sumatra, the religion spread to Java and to many other parts of the archipelago.

Conflicts arose between Islamic groups and the Hindu-Buddhist dynasties (families of rulers) on the islands. Often the royalty and nobles (wealthy landowners) from a kingdom became Muslims long before the rest of the population accepted the Islamic faith.

Majapahit Kingdom

In addition to conflicts between Muslim and Hindu-Buddhist states, the Javanese kingdoms often competed with one another for control of territory. For example, under the leadership of Prince Vijaya, the Singasari kingdom defeated an attacking army from the small Javanese kingdom of Kediri in 1293. About the same time, the prince successfully resisted Chinese advances. As a result of these victories, Vijaya emerged as ruler of Singasari. The realm entered a new era and became known as the Majapahit kingdom.

In the following decades, the Majapahit kingdom grew to be one of the most powerful and far-reaching in Indonesian history. Successive monarchs, assisted by the able military commander Gajah Mada and a growing demand for Indonesian spices from abroad, gradually expanded their realm until it claimed control over much of the archipelago.

From 1330 until his death thirty-four years later, Gajah Mada worked to unify and expand the Majapahit kingdom. Under Hayam Wuruk, who reigned from 1350 to 1389, Majapahit reached its greatest

Majapahit's rise as a great power in the fourteenth century was linked to Europe and China's growing demand for Indonesian spices. The most popular exports included nutmeg, mace, and cloves from Maluku, as well as pepper from Sumatra and western Java. Indonesian spices were used to enhance flavor in food, to preserve food, and as treatment for illnesses. The Majapahit kingdom's merchants purchased the spices from growers and brought them back to Javanese ports to be shipped to China and Europe.

height in wealth, stability, and territory. But this era, considered a golden age of Indonesian history, came to an end soon after the death of Hayam Wuruk, as smaller domains challenged Majapahit's rule in the early 1400s.

The fifteenth century was also marked by the further spread of Islam, as one community after another adopted the Muslim faith. In most cases, Indonesians mingled their Hindu and Buddhist beliefs with Islam to create a unique hybrid religion.

Europeans Arrive

In the 1500s, Europeans began entering the region to trade. Soon European powers sought to control Indonesia's profitable trade routes. The Portuguese were the first to challenge the sultans (Muslim rulers) who governed the archipelago's trade routes. In 1511 Afonso de Albuquerque and his Portuguese fleet overcame the kingdom of Melaka, which at that time controlled the flow of commerce along the Strait of Melaka. The Portuguese made alliances with sultans in the Maluku Islands to the east and engaged in trade throughout the sixteenth century. Sultans from Java repeatedly attacked the Portuguese but never won these battles against their better-armed foes.

Later in that century, other European powers—particularly the Netherlands—challenged Portuguese authority in Asian commerce. Dutch ships first entered Indonesian waters in 1596. In 1602 the government of the Netherlands approved the founding of the Dutch East India Company to trade for spices in the archipelago. The Dutch government gave this private company the authority to make treaties with Indonesians and approved military force to promote trade.

In 1610 the Dutch set up a commercial center at the Javanese city of Jayakarta (modern-day Jakarta), which they renamed Batavia. Nine years later, Jan Pieterzoon Coen became governor-general of the trading company. Coen ruthlessly pursued Dutch commercial interests, sometimes killing or deporting people who refused to sell their spices exclusively to the Dutch East India Company.

This painting shows the city of **Batavia** in the late eighteenth century. A thriving Javanese port city, Batavia was the capital of the Dutch East Indies.

The Second Mataram Kingdom and Shifts in European Control

Meanwhile, an Islamic kingdom had developed in central Java. It took the name Mataram, after the kingdom that had occupied the region centuries before. Mataram grew slowly until 1625, when the kingdom's Sultan Agung and his troops took over the powerful city of Surabaya on the northern coast of Java. Agung's power spread throughout most of central Java. His advance stopped in Batavia in 1629, when the Dutch navy defeated the sultan's forces.

Until his death in 1646, Agung defended his holdings in central and eastern Java from local nobles who wanted to claim Mataram for themselves. After he died, Agung's potential successors clashed. The Dutch took advantage of the situation by giving military support to leaders who made favorable trade agreements.

Through the middle of the 1700s, three conflicts over Mataram grew into full-scale wars of succession. The last of these wars began in 1746 and ended with the Treaty of Giyanti in 1755. The treaty split the kingdom of Mataram into a sultanate (territory controlled by a sultan) at Solo in central Java and another one at Yogyakarta on the southern coast. The division weakened Mataram, enabling the Dutch to increase their political and economic power in the region.

Soon after the separation of Mataram, Dutch leaders tried to take over the spice market. Their attempt backfired, however. Dutch trade agreements with the islands cut off British and French access to the Malukus and other spice-bearing islands. This limitation forced European merchants to establish different sources of supply. Consequently, new spice-growing regions outside of Indonesia soon overtook the archipelago's trade. Indonesian producers, who could no longer compete in the spice market, began to rely on textiles, coffee, and tea as their primary exports.

Meanwhile, events in Europe affected Indonesia. In 1795 French troops occupied the Netherlands. In 1806 Napoleon Bonaparte, who had become emperor of France, placed his brother on the Dutch throne, and the Dutch government was forced to flee the country to live in exile. French forces soon arrived in Indonesia. In an attempt to guard its colonial territory in Southeast Asia, the Dutch government-in-exile temporarily allowed Great Britain to control Dutch colonies.

In 1811 the British defeated the French forces on Java and on other islands in the archipelago. The British sent Thomas Stamford Raffles to take charge of the territory, and he made basic changes in the way the colony was run. Under the Dutch, local rulers had governed their own people. Raffles centralized authority in Batavia and divided the colony into several units. As a result of Raffles's reorganization plan, the sultans and other traditional leaders lost much of their power.

The Java War and Dutch Administration

When French domination of the Netherlands ended, the Dutch regained control of their colony from the British. Returning to Java in 1816, the Dutch faced many resentful island leaders who had lost their authority under Raffles. The Dutch had chosen not to renew the East India Company's charter, and thereafter, the government of the Netherlands formally administered the colony.

Tensions between Javanese leaders and Dutch colonial officials erupted into the Java War (1825–1830). The Dutch had continued many of the British reforms (including changes in land use and ownership) that had led to a centralized colonial government. As a result, farmers paid their rents to the central government in Batavia instead of to local nobles. The Javanese leaders were angry about losing their authority as well as a portion of their rental income.

In addition, the early 1820s saw a series of bad harvests, an epidemic of the disease cholera, and a devastating eruption of Mount Merapi near Yogyakarta. These events added to the hardship of Javanese peasantry and increased their anger toward the Dutch. Dutch insensitivity to Islamic ways also fanned the resentment of the Muslim population. One confrontation was sparked when the Dutch built a road through a Yogyakarta noble's land on which there was an Islamic tomb. Prince Diponegoro, the offended noble, became the leader of a Javanese resistance movement.

The uprisings that occurred in 1825 in central Java surprised the Dutch, who did not take the feelings of the local population very seriously. At first, the Javanese forces had considerable success. But the Dutch began to construct small forts in those areas where they had gained control. From these defensive sites, they held the colonial territories.

The conflict weakened when the rebels began to compete among themselves for power. Government forces captured Prince Diponegoro in 1830 and exiled him to Sulawesi. Many of the towns, villages, and farms of central Java were destroyed during the war. About 200,000 Indonesians died in the fighting, while Dutch losses were small in comparison.

After the Java War, the Dutch changed the centralized form of government that the British had introduced. The Dutch returned much authority to the local nobles. This move gained the loyalty of local leaders and the cooperation of the people of the archipelago. The administration of the islands was carried out on two levels, with Europeans on the top level and Indonesian nobles with their village leaders on the second tier. Dutch assistants were assigned to the nobles to represent the central government in local affairs.

Joannes van den Bosch, the Dutch governor-general of the region from 1830 to 1834, introduced a method of taxation called the Cultivation System. Under this plan, local leaders directed each village to plant certain crops on one-fifth of the land. Farmers sold their products to government merchants at a preset price. Nobles and village leaders took a percentage of the value of the crops.

Under the Cultivation System, the sale of coffee, indigo (a plant from which blue dye is made), tea, and sugar brought great profits to the Netherlands. Difficulties arose, however, when government officials

EFFECTS OF THE CULTIVATION SYSTEM

The Cultivation System forced Indonesian farmers to spend much of their time and energy on growing crops for sale instead of for food. As a result, starvation was rampant. One Dutch colonial official described the situation in 1835:

"On the roads as well as the plantations one does not meet people but only walking skeletons, which drag themselves with great difficulty from one place to another, often dying in the process. The Regent [district official] of Sukapura told me that some of the labourers who work in the plantation are in such a state of exhaustion that they die almost immediately after they have eaten from the food which is delivered to them as an advance payment for the produce to be delivered later."

—Colin Brown, *A Short History of Indonesia: The Unlikely Nation?* (Crows Nest, New South Wales, AU: Allen & Unwin, 2003), 86.

forced farmers to use more of their land to raise crops intended for the Dutch markets. As a result, rice production fell, and many people did not have enough to eat. Some regions of the country experienced famine in the 1840s and 1850s.

In 1860 Dutch author Eduard Dekker wrote the novel *Max Havelaar*, in which he exposed the greed of Dutch government officials and Indonesian nobles. The story explained how colonial policies hurt most Indonesians. When the Dutch people in the Netherlands read about the harsh conditions under which many islanders lived, they directed the Dutch legislature to change the Cultivation System.

As a result, by 1866 tea, indigo, and certain other agricultural products were no longer planted as cash-earning crops. Sugar and coffee, however, were still grown for that purpose. Dutch officials viewed these two crops as too profitable to be taken out of production quickly.

The Cultivation System was only one of the issues that angered Indonesians. Throughout the nineteenth century, the Dutch faced uprisings on Java and on many of the other islands. One group of Muslims wanted Islamic principles to govern their territory. Other villagers confronted the government, demanding more food.

By about 1900, Dutch leaders had established the Ethical Policy, which returned some of the wealth taken from the islanders through centuries of Dutch commerce. Officials in Batavia provided more health-care services, which halted outbreaks of such diseases as the bubonic plague and beriberi. The Dutch also built several schools.

Political Parties Form

Although the Dutch had changed some of their policies, many groups seeking independence for Indonesia emerged at the beginning of the twentieth century. Students in medical training founded the Budi Utomo (Noble Endeavor Society) in 1908, and its leaders spoke out forcefully against continued Dutch control of the islands. The Indies Party, which began meeting in 1912, also called for independence from the Netherlands. The Dutch quickly outlawed this organization and exiled its leaders. Muslim traders founded Sarekat Islam (Islamic Union), which promoted the principles of Islam. This group also attempted to weaken the economic influence of Chinese merchants who had immigrated to the islands.

By 1924 the Indonesian Communist Party (known as PKI from the initials of its Indonesian name) was gaining wide support among members of workers' organizations. In 1926 the Communists started a revolt in Java and Sumatra, but Dutch troops quickly overcame the rebels.

The Dutch banned the PKI and sent its leaders out of the country. During the next twenty years, the PKI had a very small membership.

In 1927 Sukarno, a young civil engineer who, like many Javanese, was identified by a single name, formed the Indonesian Nationalist Party (PNI). The party based its call for national independence on Islamic principles and traditional beliefs. Sukarno's stirring speeches expressed the feelings of many islanders, and his appeal attracted many members to the PNI. The Dutch banned the PNI and in 1929 put Sukarno in jail for two years.

Sultan Sjahrir and Muhammad Hatta began another nationalist group in 1931, and their party platform focused on providing education for the population. In 1934 Hatta was arrested and sent into exile. Hatta was kept isolated for eight years, along with Sukarno, who had been sent away again a year later.

World War II and Postwar Developments

As Indonesia's internal conflicts continued, World War II (1939–1945) brewed in the Pacific. Japanese forces began taking over territories in eastern Asia in the 1930s. By 1942 the Allied troops of the United States and Britain, along with the Netherlands, were fighting the Japanese army and navy.

The Japanese wanted to conquer Indonesia in order to control the Strait of Melaka. This sea-lane provided access to the Indian Ocean and to Indonesia's natural resources, notably oil and rubber. The Japanese Imperial Navy defeated the Allied forces in the Battle of the Java Sea on February 27, 1942. The next month, the Dutch surrendered and the Japanese occupied the islands.

To gain the support of Indonesians, the Japanese allowed Sukarno, Hatta, and other nationalists—whom the Dutch had exiled—to return to Java. Many nationalists aided the Japanese in the hope of eventually achieving independence. Other Indonesians found Japanese rule too harsh and refused to cooperate.

During the three years of Japanese control, the occupiers allowed some Indonesians to participate in the administration of the islands. The Japanese also trained an Indonesian army of more than 50,000 soldiers to protect the colony from attack by the Allies. Other Indonesians did not fare as well. About 250,000 were sent to other Japanese-occupied territories as an unpaid labor force. More than half of these workers died from the difficult living and working conditions that the Japanese imposed.

In 1944 the war was beginning to turn against Japan. Nevertheless, the Japanese allowed the Indonesians to make plans for independence.

Sukarno, Hatta, and others organized the new government through mid-1945, when it became clear that Japan could not win the war. The territory of the proposed nation included all the islands of the archipelago as well as the Malay Peninsula.

On June 1, 1945, Sukarno made a speech outlining five principles, or Pancasila (a Sanskrit word), to guide the new nation. Sukarno's five guidelines were humanitarianism (a belief in social reform for the good of all), national unity, representative government, social justice, and belief in one God. Pancasila caught the imagination of many Indonesians and still forms a basis for organizing the nation.

Soon after Sukarno's Pancasila speech, the Japanese surrendered to the Allies on August 15, 1945. Indonesian nationalists declared independence two days later. Sukarno became president, and Hatta assumed the role of vice president. By the time the British, as Allied representatives, arrived on September 29, the leaders of the archipelago had created an army and had established many governmental offices. But the British and the Indonesian nationalists could not agree on the future of the country.

In late October, the tension between British troops stationed in Java and the Indonesian army flared into violence. In Surabaya a large Indonesian force attacked the British, who launched their own attack and overcame the Indonesians after several weeks of fighting. Although the Indonesian forces were defeated, the effort unified the people and strengthened their desire for nationhood.

After the British victory, the Dutch returned and tried to regain control of the territory. In November 1946, the Dutch recognized local Indonesian authority by signing the Linggajati Agreement with nationalist leaders. But the accord also gave the Dutch a legal right to remain on Java and on some of the other islands. In July 1947, the Dutch army attacked Indonesian troops on Sumatra and Java to gain territory. The Europeans occupied large areas formerly held by Indonesians.

The United Nations protested the Dutch expansion. When the Dutch again attacked Indonesian positions, the UN demanded that the Dutch withdraw. World opinion was also against the Dutch, who hoped to obtain international aid to rebuild the Netherlands after the war. As a result, the Dutch forces withdrew from most of Indonesia. The archipelago became independent on December 27, 1949. In May 1950, the country's leaders formally organized the Republic of Indonesia.

To learn more about Indonesia's involvement in World War II, the Japanese and Dutch invasions, and Indonesia's independence, visit www.vgsbooks.com for links.

Sukarno and Suharto

After the country achieved independence, internal political differences kept the government from running smoothly. Sukarno continued as president, but other leaders found ways to limit his powers during the early years of nationhood. Sukarno's solution to this problem was a plan called Guided Democracy. In a speech in October 1956, he outlined an idealistic program of government based on consensus (general agreement), collectivism (shared work and shared economic rewards), and national unity.

The armed forces and the growing Communist Party supported Sukarno's plan. Other political groups did not, and their activities weakened the government. In 1957 Sukarno strengthened his position by proclaiming martial law (rule by military force). Two years later, he set up a new legislature with members mostly loyal to him.

Sukarno's actions did not solve the nation's major problems. Complaining of slow economic progress, Indonesians in Sumatra and Sulawesi revolted in 1958. After years of fighting, the Indonesian army defeated the rebels in 1961. During these years, Sukarno was unable to guide the country to prosperity. To stay in power, he balanced the power of the army, which was mostly anti-Communist, against the influence of Indonesia's increasingly strong PKI.

In September 1965, troops led by General Suharto, a strong anti-Communist, halted an attempted coup d'état (government overthrow) in which several generals were assassinated. Most Indonesians blamed the Communist Party for the failed coup. Its organizers wanted to reduce the army's influence but keep Sukarno in power. The army and many Islamic groups attacked Communists throughout the country during the next several months. Roughly

Muslim students burn down the Communist Youth Organization headquarters after the **failed coup attempt** in October 1965.

500,000 people died, and many others were arrested. The government banned the PKI in 1966.

With the army and many student groups supporting him, Suharto began to push Sukarno out of power. Although Sukarno remained president until 1967, he exercised little authority. Suharto officially became president in 1968.

Early in his administration, Suharto fired many government officials in order to root out corruption and to eliminate Sukarno loyalists. Suharto established closer ties with Indonesia's neighbors and settled a territorial conflict with Malaysia. He also looked to Western democratic nations for economic aid. The army remained very active in the nation's political life. High-ranking officers continued to manage the oil, mining, and forestry industries, which they had controlled since the early 1960's. Suharto chose military officers to fill half of the posts in his cabinet.

Under Suharto, Indonesia acquired two additional pieces of territory. In 1969 the local councils in Papua (known as Dutch New Guinea, later renamed Irian Jaya), which had gone from Dutch to UN supervision, chose to join Indonesia. This action, known as the Act of Free Choice, was widely criticized by Papuans because the local council members were handpicked by the Indonesian government to ensure a favorable outcome.

In turn, many Papuans have provided support and members to the Free Papua Movement, a pro-independence military group. In the years since the Act of Free Choice, the Free Papua Movement has engaged in attacks on government facilities as well as kidnappings of government officials and foreigners. The actions of the Free Papua Movement led the Indonesian government to station troops in Papua. Human rights groups have accused Indonesian soldiers of committing human rights abuses such as torture, false imprisonment, and murder against Papuans.

An even more serious human rights crisis occurred in East Timor, the eastern half of the island of Timor. Until the mid-1970s, East Timor had been a Portuguese colony. But a Portuguese decision to give up the territory led to civil war between East Timorese who sought to join Indonesia and those who favored independence. In 1975 Indonesian forces invaded East Timor to stop the civil war and, shortly thereafter, declared the region part of Indonesia.

Many East Timorese fought against this move. In response, Indonesian troops engaged in a brutal suppression campaign against the rebels. In the following decades, actions of the Indonesian military led to the deaths of about 200,000 East Timorese—approximately one-third of the population. The UN and many foreign powers strongly condemned the Indonesian government's harsh actions.

Disputes over government control also led to bloody conflict in the strongly Muslim province of Aceh on the western tip of Sumatra. Acehnese leaders opposed the Indonesian government's emphasis on Pancasila, instead preferring a government rooted in Islamic tradition and Islamic Sharia law. In 1976 a group of Acehnese declared their region's independence from Indonesia. The central government sent in troops to crush the rebels, sparking a long and costly conflict. By the late 1980s, the separatists had named themselves the Free Aceh Movement and were engaging in guerrilla attacks on government installations and businesses throughout Aceh.

Meanwhile, Suharto and his political party, Golkar, closely controlled Indonesian politics and the media. Suharto won several presidential elections, although none of the contests have been deemed free and fair by international observers.

End of the Suharto Era and the Beginning of Democracy

By the 1990s, many Indonesians and outsiders accused Suharto and his family of sponsoring rampant corruption. Allegations that the Suharto family received bribes from international companies and sold governmental favors were commonplace by the middle of the decade. As the aging leader faced mounting criticism, a financial crisis struck Asia in 1997. Indonesia was hit hardest as banks closed, businesses failed, and many Indonesians were left impoverished.

The crisis, known as the Asian Financial Crisis, led to widespread anger at the Suharto government, which appeared incapable of dealing with the crisis. In Jakarta university students held large demonstrations against the government. On May 14, 1998, troops were called in to halt the demonstrations. When the soldiers opened fire on the students, killing several, riots broke out across the country. The violence quickly escalated out of control. After a week of rioting, during which several hundred people were killed and millions of dollars in damage was caused, Suharto resigned. His vice president, B. J. Habibie, took over.

Habibie instituted a swath of reforms. They included the holding of free and fair legislative elections and allowing more freedom of the press. Habibie also allowed the population of East Timor to vote in a referendum for or against independence on August 30, 1999. The Timorese voted overwhelmingly for independence, but the results angered anti-independence Timorese. Once again, violence erupted in East Timor, and the Indonesian military was accused of siding with the anti-independence movement in a campaign against the pro-independence population. A UN peacekeeping force, led by Australian troops, was called in to end the bloodshed. Indonesian forces pulled out of the region soon after, and the Timorese began setting up their own independent government.

Meanwhile, Indonesia's economic troubles continued. By 1999 about 90 percent of the country's major corporations were technically bankrupt, and about 20 million Indonesians were unemployed. In the years following, a succession of presidents, including Megawati Sukarnoputri, daughter of the country's first president, tried to bring the economy back under control, with mixed results.

Indonesia's economic recovery was further hampered by a deadly terrorist attack in October 2002. Islamic terrorists set off two bombs in a resort on the island of Bali, killing more than two hundred people, most of them Australian tourists. The bombings were the world's deadliest terrorist attack in the wake of the September 11, 2001, attacks on the United States. The Bali incident devastated the Indonesian tourist industry, as many travelers chose to avoid the country afterward. The Bali bombings also placed the country's small militant Muslim movement into the world spotlight. Indonesian police quickly rounded up, tried, and convicted the bombers.

By the early 2000s, the Indonesian economy was enjoying some stability, and the reforms first implemented by President Habibie were taking effect. In September 2004, the first truly free and fair presidential elections were held in Indonesia, with former army general Susilo Bambang Yudhoyono emerging the victor.

The new president faces many challenges, including the armed separatist movement in Aceh. The Indonesian armed forces continued

Many Indonesians voted for **Susilo Bambang Yudhoyono** in 2004 because they saw him as a person of honesty and integrity. He won the election for president.

their effort to crush the independence movement in Aceh. After a brief cease-fire, the military launched a full-scale operation to eliminate the Free Aceh Movement. But this effort failed. The horrific disaster of the 2004 earthquake and tsunami (in which Aceh suffered the most damage) led to a temporary halt in hostilities. But a final resolution to the conflict is not imminent.

Government

Established in 1945, Indonesia's first constitution was reinstated in 1959 after a nine-year absence. Under Sukarno and Suharto, the document provided for a powerful president who appointed cabinet members, set national policy, and made most decisions free of legislative influence. Since the end of Suharto's leadership, numerous reforms have limited the power of the president. Perhaps the most important reform was a law passed in 2002 that called for presidents to be elected directly by the population. The president is allowed to serve a maximum of two five-year terms.

Indonesia has a one-thousand-member People's Consultative Assembly. This large congress meets at least once every five years to discuss national policy. The Indonesian legislature is known as the People's Representation Council and is composed of five hundred members.

The foundation of Indonesia's judicial system is the district court. The code of criminal law is the same in all areas of the country, but civil cases are tried according to local or religious custom. Islamic courts hear personal cases, which may deal with divorce or inheritance.

For administrative purposes, Indonesia is divided into 26 provinces. The president appoints a governor to rule each territory. Village councils make decisions on the local level.

THE PEOPLE

Estimates of Indonesia's population range from 222 million to 234 million people, making Indonesia the fourth most populous country in the world. Only China, India, and the United States contain larger populations. About 60 percent of Indonesians (133 million to 140 million) live on Java, making the island one of the most densely populated areas in the world. (Java's land area is about the size of the state of New York.) Other regions, such as the so-called "outer islands" of Papua, Kalimantan, Sumatra, and Sulawesi, are very sparsely populated.

The Javanese have dominated the region's history just as they stand out in the nation's population statistics. The cultural and economic center of the country, Java has been the home of most of Indonesia's leaders. In the past, the government has tried to combat overcrowding on Java—as well as on the islands of Bali, Madura, and Lombok—by resettling some of the population on the less inhabited outer islands.

Officials believed that a more balanced distribution of people and of financial resources could help the country to develop economically and

socially. However, these transmigration programs proved to be very expensive and largely unsuccessful. Meanwhile, original residents of the resettled islands greatly resented the government forcing people onto their homelands, and clashes between newcomers and indigenous peoples frequently turned violent. In addition, the transmigration program made only a small dent in the Javanese overpopulation problem. The Indonesian government officially abandoned the program in 2000.

Ethnic Groups and Language

Indonesia's population includes more than three hundred ethnic groups. Separation by seas and mountains has kept the various populations and their customs and languages distinct from one another.

The largest of the nation's ethnic groups—representing about 45 percent of the population—is the Javanese. Residing mostly in east and central Java and on part of Sumatra, the Javanese have a highly developed social structure. People of high status use a different grammar and vocabulary than do those of lower social station. The Javanese have held powerful governmental positions throughout Indonesian history, but most members of this ethnic group are tenant farmers who live in villages. Although the majority of Javanese are Muslims, pre-Islamic rituals—such as the *slametan* feast, meant to promote contentment—are still central to Javanese life.

Another ethnic group, the Sundanese, also live on Java, with most inhabiting the western part of the island. They make up about 14 percent of the population, and many are rice farmers. The Sundanese are Muslims who carefully fulfill the Islamic duties of daily prayer and a yearly fast. The social structure of the Sundanese people is much simpler than that of their Javanese neighbors.

The Madurese, most of whom live on the island of Madura off the northeastern coast of Java, represent about 7.5 percent of Indonesia's population. These Muslims generally live in traditional villages of about three hundred to one thousand inhabitants. In past decades, many Madurese participated in the transmigration program, moving from their home island to other parts of the country.

The Malay form about 7.5 percent of the population. Most live on Sumatra and the small island of Riau off Sumatra's northern coast. Indonesia's Malay share traditional ties with the people of neighboring Malaysia and were the founders of the old Buddhist kingdom of Srivijaya. In modern times, most Malay are Muslims, and a form of the Malay language, Bahasa Indonesia, has become the official language of Indonesia.

The national motto of Indonesia is *Bhinneka tunggal ika*, which roughly translates to "Unity in Diversity." The phrase celebrates the country's unity while highlighting Indonesia's varied range of peoples.

About 3 percent of the population are ethnic Chinese. During the colonial era, many of them served as merchants under the Dutch. In modern times, ethnic Chinese control much of the country's wealth—perhaps as much as 80 percent of the economy—through banks, shops, industries, hotels, and restaurants. Because of this economic imbalance, Chinese face deep resentment and prejudice from other Indonesians. Under Suharto, the Indonesian government made it illegal to publish works in Chinese or to teach Chinese languages in schools. Public celebrations of the Chinese New Year were also banned. Most recently, the Jakarta riots of 1998 focused their anger on the Chinese, and many Chinese citizens were murdered in the wave of violence. Since the fall of Suharto, the government has eased restrictions on Chinese culture, allowing public celebrations of the Chinese New Year and allowing

Chinese-language newspapers and magazines to be published. Teaching the Chinese language in school remains illegal, however.

Hundreds of other ethnic groups make up the remaining 23 percent of Indonesia's population. Among them are the Acehnese in northern Sumatra and the Minangkabau in the central region of Sumatra. Both of these Muslim groups grow rice to make a living. They share the island with the Bataks, most of whom are either Christians or Muslims. Bataks allow only members of the same clan to live together in a village. Members of a Batak village collectively own the farmland. At harvesttime, the village council distributes portions of the produce to farmers and their families.

On Kalimantan many Dayaks live in remote areas in dwellings called longhouses. Several hundred feet long, these structures accommodate dozens of families, each having a separate room. In the past, the Dayaks responded violently to the government's transmigration efforts by attacking newcomers to their region. Another ethnic group, the Buginese, were sea traders who for centuries ventured from Sulawesi to many ocean destinations. B. J. Habibie, Indonesia's third president, is a member of the Buginese ethnic group. The Christian Ambonese from the Malukus became known for their military organization. Dutch colonizers often hired them to fight on the side of the Netherlands in regional conflicts.

The people who probably have the least in common with other Indonesian ethnic groups are the Papuans. They share more characteristics with their neighbors in Papua New Guinea than with other

Many older **Dayak** women are distinguished by their stretched earlobes, a practice less common with younger generations. **Indigenous Papuans** are very diverse, and some estimate that between 200 and 700 different languages are spoken on the island.

Bahasa Indonesia

In 1928 the Indonesian independence movement gave the title Bahasa Indonesia to the Malay language that was spoken widely throughout the archipelago. The language's appeal stems from its wide use and relative simplicity. Virtually all Indonesian schoolchildren learn Bahasa Indonesia, although most schools rely on local languages for the first three years of a child's school career. In 1972 Indonesia and Malaysia strengthened ties by adopting revised spellings of their official languages. These changes helped to make the two languages more similar, allowing for better communication between the two countries.

Indonesians. Both groups have a Melanesian ancestry. The language, customs, and religious practices of the Papuans are similar to those of indigenous peoples in Australia and on the islands of Melanesia, east of New Guinea.

Indonesia's official language is an offshoot of the Malay tongue. Like English, Bahasa Indonesia is written in the Latin alphabet. Indonesia's national language also contains Dutch, Portuguese, and Arabic words. Used at official functions and on many public occasions, Bahasa Indonesia is one of several Malayo-Polynesian tongues spoken in the archipelago. Many Indonesians can communicate in two or more of the nation's 25 languages, which are spoken in more than 250 distinct dialects.

Most Javanese people speak their own tongue at home, as do the Sundanese and other Indonesian ethnic groups. During the first three years of school, the language of each region is used during instruction. Bahasa Indonesia is spoken beginning in grade four. English is often taught in secondary school.

Education

Aside from schools for the wealthy, very few opportunities for education existed in Indonesia prior to independence in 1949. In 1950 the Indonesian government set a goal that all Indonesian children should receive at least six years of education. Although this goal has not been met, the vast majority of Indonesian children ages seven to twelve do attend elementary school. However, even elementary schooling is not free for students, and many poor families struggle to afford tuition, books, and uniforms. About 88 percent of Indonesians over the age of fifteen are literate—meaning they are able to read and write—with more males being literate (92 percent) than females (83 percent).

Although most Indonesian elementary schools receive some public funding, many families choose to pay to send their children to private

Children from the Dani tribe attend school in central Papua.

schools. These schools are generally considered to be of higher quality. While state-run schools stress the importance of Pancasila, the majority of private schools emphasize Muslim teachings. Many of these institutions are operated by mosques.

Following six years of elementary school, just over half the country's students move on to secondary school. The secondary school program is divided into three years of junior high education, followed by three more years of senior high. Only a small percentage of Indonesians go on to attend college. Most of Indonesia's universities are located on Java. The University of Indonesia, with two campuses on Java, is the country's largest institution of higher education. The school offers courses on a variety of subjects, including law, medicine, dentistry, psychology, political science, economics, public health, and engineering.

To learn more about Indonesia's many ethnic groups, their languages, and their schools, including the University of Indonesia, the country's largest university, visit www.vgsbooks.com for links.

Health

As a generally poor country—roughly half the population lives in poverty—Indonesia struggles with substandard nutrition, lack of sanitation, and a shortage of medical services.

In recent decades, however, Indonesia has made significant strides in improving the health of its citizens. Over the last thirty years, life expectancy for Indonesians has risen from 42 to 65 years, while the infant mortality rate (the number of children who die in their first year) has dropped from 140 per 1,000 live births to 48 per 1,000 live births. These successes are partly due to government immunization programs, which have helped to drastically reduce (although not completely wipe out) outbreaks of such preventable diseases as measles, diphtheria, and polio. Other preventable diseases, such as malaria, have been largely eradicated on Java but remain a significant problem on other islands.

Yet despite these accomplishments, Indonesia's health-care system still struggles to meet the needs of the population. A recent study states that there are 1,145 hospitals in Indonesia but that at least 600 more are needed. Indonesia does not have a national health insurance system, and many citizens do not have private insurance. Thus, many Indonesians, particularly poor people, cannot afford the high cost of medical treatment. Other challenges to the health-care system include a lack of medical equipment and a lack of materials for the production of medicines.

Poverty is also a key factor in Indonesia's high rate of malnutrition, especially among children. As many as one-quarter of all Indonesian children are underweight, meaning they consume an inadequate diet. In many cases, malnutrition leads to other health problems, including stuntedness (incomplete growth) and increased vulnerability to disease.

Crowded conditions and a lack of sanitation services have also had a negative effect on the health of many Indonesians. For example, an estimated 90 percent of Jakarta's water wells are contaminated with disease-carrying bacteria, and most citizens must either boil water or purchase bottled water to have clean water to drink. Air pollution is also a significant problem in the larger cities such as Jakarta and has led to an increase in respiratory illnesses such as asthma and emphysema.

The earthquake and resulting tsunami of late 2004 had a devastating effect on the health of Indonesians on Sumatra. Among the 122,000 killed

LEAD POISONING

Air pollution created by the use of leaded gasoline in Indonesian vehicles has become a serious health threat to the nation's children. Lead poisoning can cause a number of developmental problems in children. A recent study by the U.S. Centers for Disease Control and Prevention found that more than one-third of Indonesian children had blood lead levels high enough to be considered a danger to their developmental health.

and 114,000 missing were hundreds of medical personnel, many of whom were swept away along with their hospitals and clinics. Although generous international aid is assisting victims and helping them to rebuild the island's health-care services, experts believe it will take years for the region to recover. On a positive note, massive outbreaks of disease, feared by many observers in the aftermath of the disaster, failed to materialize.

The government's longstanding family planning program was implemented to slow the rate of population growth. Of 5,000 established clinics, 3,000 are located on Java and Bali. Focusing on educating people at every level of society, local field-workers go door-to-door and provide information and medical services. The program has been largely successful in curbing the birth rate, and more than half of Indonesian women use some form of contraception. In the early 1970s, the average Indonesian woman had six to seven children. This number has dropped to about three children per woman in the early 2000s. However, although the population is increasing at a slower rate as a result of this program, some estimates state that the country's population will reach 400 million by 2040.

The global HIV/AIDS epidemic has not spared Indonesia. Recent statistics state that 110,000 Indonesians have either the human immunodeficiency virus (HIV) or the disease that it causes, acquired immunodeficiency syndrome (AIDS). Indonesian public health officials are working to educate the public about the dangers of HIV/AIDS and how to prevent the spread of the disease.

As part of Indonesia's ongoing **family planning program,** billboards around the country advocate the use of birth control for limiting family sizes.

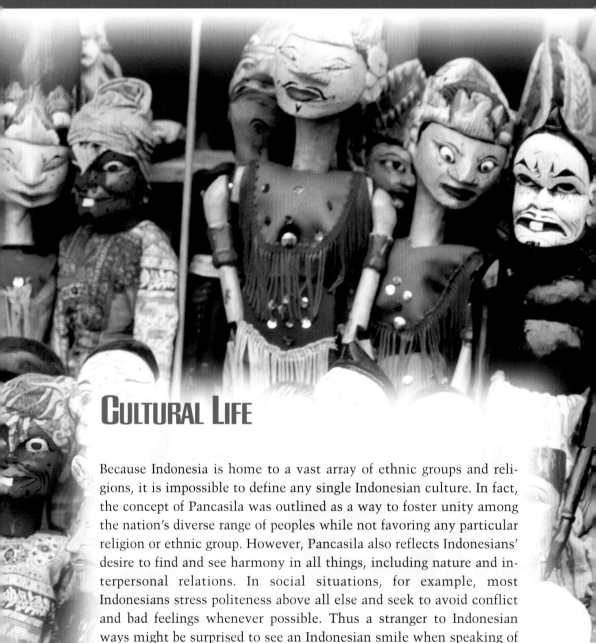

CULTURAL LIFE

Because Indonesia is home to a vast array of ethnic groups and religions, it is impossible to define any single Indonesian culture. In fact, the concept of Pancasila was outlined as a way to foster unity among the nation's diverse range of peoples while not favoring any particular religion or ethnic group. However, Pancasila also reflects Indonesians' desire to find and see harmony in all things, including nature and interpersonal relations. In social situations, for example, most Indonesians stress politeness above all else and seek to avoid conflict and bad feelings whenever possible. Thus a stranger to Indonesian ways might be surprised to see an Indonesian smile when speaking of a sad event—such as a death in the family—but the smile is intended to maintain harmony by not burdening strangers with personal affairs.

▶ Religion

Early Indonesians practiced various forms of animism. Animism is the worship of spirits that are believed to live in all things, from trees and

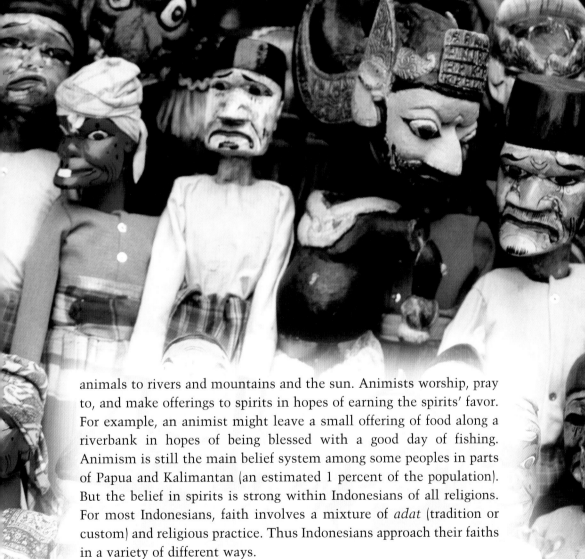

animals to rivers and mountains and the sun. Animists worship, pray to, and make offerings to spirits in hopes of earning the spirits' favor. For example, an animist might leave a small offering of food along a riverbank in hopes of being blessed with a good day of fishing. Animism is still the main belief system among some peoples in parts of Papua and Kalimantan (an estimated 1 percent of the population). But the belief in spirits is strong within Indonesians of all religions. For most Indonesians, faith involves a mixture of *adat* (tradition or custom) and religious practice. Thus Indonesians approach their faiths in a variety of different ways.

Indonesia is the world's largest Muslim country. About 88 percent of Indonesians are Muslims. Islam was founded in the Arabian Peninsula in the 600s and spread to other parts of the world in the following centuries. Indian and Arab Muslims carried their faith to the archipelago, and the religion became widespread in Indonesia starting in the thirteenth century.

Duties of Muslims include praying daily, fasting, and giving money to the poor. Once in their lifetime, male Muslims try to make a pilgrimage (religious journey) to the holy city of Mecca in Saudi Arabia—the birthplace of Islam.

Generally speaking, Indonesian Islam is much less formal and rigid than the Islam practiced in other parts of the world, such as the Middle East. For example, few Indonesians pray five times a day, as called for in the Quran (the holy book of Islam), although most do participate in the Friday noon prayer. Some Indonesian traditions, such as the worship of saints, continue despite being forbidden under Islamic law. Muslim practice also differs from region to region. Thus Acehnese tend to be stricter Muslims, while urban dwellers on Java and Sumatra tend to follow a looser form of the faith.

Christians make up about 8 percent of the Indonesian population, with about 5 percent Protestant and 3 percent Catholic. In the sixteenth century, Portuguese traders who traveled to the Malukus for spices brought Christian missionaries to the area. The first Christian missionaries were Portuguese Roman Catholics. After the Dutch took over the islands, missionaries came from Protestant churches in the Netherlands. Christian congregations are biggest on the Malukus but also are found in Sumatra, Timor, and Kalimantan. Like their fellow Muslim citizens, Indonesian Christians often mix their beliefs and rituals with animist and Hindu-Buddhist beliefs and rituals.

About 3 percent of the Indonesian population are Hindu, Buddhist, or a combination of the two. Indian travelers carried the Hindu religion to the archipelago during ancient times, with Buddhism arriving from the Asian mainland at about the same time. By the ninth century A.D., many Javanese nobles were practicing the religions and slowly combining the two faiths into a hybrid form. In turn, when Islam and Christianity began to take hold on the islands, they combined with Hinduism, Buddhism, and animism.

SEMANGAT

Many Indonesians believe that supernatural life forces live within all beings as well as certain sacred objects. These forces are known as *semangat*. The semangat of human beings is believed to lie in a person's head and hair. Because of this, Indonesians consider it very rude to touch a person's head.

Certain important life ceremonies involve hair. For example, Indonesian babies receive a ceremonial first haircut as an initiation into society. During weddings, the hair of the bride and groom are often knotted together. Hair clippings are usually disposed of carefully to keep them from falling into the hands of an evil sorcerer.

In modern times, the island of Bali is home to the largest mixed Hindu-Buddhist population in Indonesia. Hinduism and Buddhism both encourage people to seek wisdom and truth. Balinese religious practices highlight peaceful living in personal, social, and political life. The majority of Indonesian Buddhists are ethnic Chinese.

Folk Arts and Crafts

Indonesians combine music and drama with highly developed folk arts when they celebrate religious and regional festivals. Several kinds of *wayang* (shadow plays) are often the central activity during these gatherings. Some wayang use puppets—either flat, cutout forms made of pressed leather or three-dimensional objects carved from wood—to cast shadows on a large screen made of white cloth. In other wayang performances, dancers enact stories without a screen. Wayang plays often last through the night, and audiences pay close attention even as they move around and talk quietly.

The dramas of the wayang often portray the battle between good and evil in the lives of gods and heroes. The *Ramayana* of Indian Hindu origin is often the source of wayang plots, especially for performances on the island of Bali. Wayang provide not only entertainment but also common national symbols that politicians, religious leaders, and others in public life use to communicate their ideas.

Wayang performances, dances, and other village entertainments are accompanied by an Indonesian orchestra called a gamelan. Musicians in this age-old musical assembly play drums, metal bars (which are struck like xylophones), gongs, stringed instruments, and bamboo flutes.

Most temple festivals on Bali include dances. A common character is **the Barong *(left)*, a mischievous half-lion, half-dog creature** that represents good and protects the village from the *rangda*, or witch.

Gamelan are found throughout Indonesia. Even in small villages, local people contribute to the purchase and upkeep of instruments for their gamelan. Ethnic groups from various regions feature different instruments, giving Indonesian gamelan many distinctive sounds.

Indonesian crafts reflect the wide range of histories and cultures of the archipelago's far-flung peoples. Crafts originating in Java and Bali (the so-called "inner islands") tend to be heavily influenced by Hindu-Buddhist traditions. For example, Balinese artisans work with *paras*, a soft, ashy limestone to produce beautiful carved statues of Hindu gods. Arts of the so-called "outer islands," such as Sumatra, Kalimantan, Sulawesi, and Papua, are more strongly influenced by animist traditions. Such traditions can be seen in the works of the Dayak people of Kalimantan, who carve *hampatong*, large, carved wooden poles that serve as guardians against evil spirits.

Islamic art has also lent its influence to Indonesian crafts. Although much of Indonesian art does not follow the rules of Islam that forbid human and animal representation, Indonesians have incorporated the elaborate designs and patterns of Islamic art into their works.

Other beautiful and unique crafts can be found throughout Indonesia, both in cities and in the countryside. Textiles are perhaps the best-known Indonesian crafts. Artisans weave, embroider, and dye cloth to make costumes for dancers and musicians. Batik is a dyeing process that results in intricately patterned and colored cloth. Dyers put wax on the parts of the material that they want to keep free of a particular color of dye. Many applications of wax and dye—sometimes taking months—may be used in the batik-making process.

Indonesians have been making **batik cloth (*right*)** for many centuries—possibly as early as the twelfth century. The word *batik* is Javanese for "to dot." To learn more about the Indonesian art of batik, visit www.vgsbooks.com for links.

Children wave Indonesian flags during **Independence Day** celebrations outside the presidential palace in Jakarta.

◗ Holidays and Festivals

Most Indonesian holidays and festivals are centered on religious occasions, but one particular secular (nonreligious) occasion unites people of all faiths—Independence Day. Falling on August 17, Independence Day is celebrated with parades and dancing. Another important secular holiday is Kartini Day (April 21). The event celebrates Raden Ajeng Kartini (1879–1904), one of the country's most honored heroes. Kartini worked tirelessly for her country's independence and for the rights of Indonesian women. She was also a powerful advocate for equal education for all Indonesian women. Kartini Day is celebrated with parades, lectures, and school activities,. Women are given a break from their traditional chores, while fathers and children pitch in to do the household work.

Islamic holidays dominate Indonesia's calendar, reflecting the country's Muslim majority. Because the Islamic calendar is based on the 354-day lunar year instead of the 365-day Gregorian calendar used in the West, the dates of festivals fall back about 11 days every year.

To honor God and to test their self-discipline, Muslims do not eat or drink from dawn to dusk during the holy month of Ramadan. Once the sun sets each evening, people gather to eat after a long day of fasting. The end of Ramadan culminates in the biggest and most important festival of the year, Lebaran (or Idul Fitri). For this two-day event, Indonesians dress in their finest clothes, light firecrackers, and enjoy elaborate meals. Families gather to celebrate, ask forgiveness from their elders for any sins they may have committed during the past year, and visit the graves to honor their deceased relatives.

Garebeg is another important Islamic holiday. It marks the birth of the prophet Muhammad, the founder of Islam. For this holiday, Muslims prepare large ceremonial food mounds. These are then carried to each city or town's main mosque. The food is later blessed and distributed to worshippers. The blessed food, known as *gunungan*, is believed to bring good fortune and good harvest to those who eat it. Other Islamic holidays include Isra Mi'raj Nabi Muhammad, or the Ascension of the prophet Muhammad, celebrating the night when Muhammad was brought to heaven to speak to Allah (God); Hegira, the Islamic New Year, which marks Muhammad's trip from Mecca to Medina (both in Saudi Arabia) to start a new Muslim community there; and Idul Adha, a festival during which Muslims sacrifice goats and cattle to honor Abraham's willingness to sacrifice his son, as told in the Bible.

Indonesia's other religious communities also mark important days with exciting festivals and feasts. The biggest Hindu celebration is Nyepi, or the Hindu New Year. It is celebrated most widely on

Muslim women gather at a mosque in Aceh Province to pray on Idul Adha.

Bali. While the day itself (which falls in March or April) is spent in the complete silence of prayer and meditation, the day before is marked by loud and joyous celebrations. The celebrations are believed to scare off evil spirits. The following day of silence is meant to keep the spirits away by fooling them into thinking that the community is deserted.

Waisak (May 7) is the most important Buddhist festival. It celebrates the birth, moment of enlightenment, and death of Buddha. In the largest Waisak ceremony, Buddhist monks gather at the Borobudur Temple to recite prayers and make offerings. Among Christian festivals, Easter and Christmas are the most important. The island of Flores is famous for its solemn Easter observance, when Christians march barefoot through the island's streets at midnight carrying torches and candles.

Food

A dizzying array of outside influences have shaped Indonesia's unique cuisine. The ancient Malay brought rice and the art of stir-frying—quickly cooking vegetables and meat in a bowl-shaped pan called a wok. Visitors and immigrants from India introduced cooking with the spices curry and turmeric, and Arab traders brought recipes for sheep dishes and kabobs—meat and vegetable skewers that Indonesians enjoy as *sate*. Visitors and conquerors from Europe passed along such vegetables as carrots and tomatoes.

The variety of Indonesian cuisine also reflects the diversity of the country's population. Although certain basic ingredients are used throughout most of the archipelago, the people on each island bring a unique twist to their own regional cuisine.

Nearly all Indonesian dishes contain one or a combination of the following key ingredients: rice, coconuts, bananas, peanuts, and soybeans. Rice is the staple food of Indonesia and is served with virtually every meal. The archipelago produces several different kinds of rice, including white rice, sticky white rice, red rice, yellow rice, and sticky black rice. Among the most popular dishes is *nasi goreng*—fried rice with an assortment of vegetables and/or meat.

INDONESIAN MEALS

Indonesians typically eat two meals a day with snack times in between. Meals in Indonesian homes tend to be nonsocial activities. Food is often cooked in the morning and left on the kitchen table for the day. Family members just help themselves to a meal whenever they are hungry. Family mealtime gatherings tend to take place only on holidays or during feasts.

PISANG GORENG

Fried bananas are a delicious and popular dessert or snack in Indonesia. Indonesians often purchase them made to order from street vendors. For best results, serve immediately after cooking, when the crust is crisp and the fruit is soft and warm. Be sure an adult is present whenever you cook with hot oil.

¾ cup flour	4 small, ripe bananas
½ teaspoon salt	1 cup canola oil for frying
¾ to 1 cup water	1 tablespoon sugar
1 lime, zested and cut into wedges	

1. In a medium bowl, combine flour and salt.
2. Add enough water to make a smooth batter that is somewhat thick. Add lime zest and mix well.
3. Peel bananas and dip them in the batter two or three times, until well coated.
4. In a deep skillet, heat oil to 375°F (190°C) or until a piece of bread browns in 30 seconds. (Use a kitchen thermometer to check the temperature of the oil.)
5. Place bananas in the oil slowly and carefully. Fry two at a time, until they are crisp and golden brown. Remove with a slotted spoon and place on paper towels to absorb the oil.
6. To serve, arrange bananas on a plate and sprinkle with sugar. Garnish with lime wedges.

Serves 4

Coconut and coconut oil are very important to Indonesian cuisine. Most Indonesians use coconut oil for cooking, and coconut milk adds flavor to many soups and curries. Coconut is also found in many sweets, and grated coconut is often added to vegetable dishes. Bananas grow in many different sizes in Indonesia and are eaten baked, boiled, or fried. Indonesians eat banana flowers, and even banana leaves are used as wrapping material for steamed meat, fish, and vegetables.

Peanuts are often mixed in vegetable dishes, while sweet and spicy peanut sauce is served with sate, salads, and many other foods. Soybeans are another staple food of Indonesia and a key source of protein. The beans are usually served as cake (*tempe*), or as soybean curd, or tofu (*tahu*). Soybean leaves are also consumed as vegetables. The wide variety of spices that grow on the archipelago include cloves, lemongrass, coriander, pepper, and garlic.

Most Indonesians eat relatively little meat. But seafood—shrimp, in particular—is popular, as well as beef.

Literature and Media

In ancient times, Indonesians passed on traditions and life lessons through folktales. These stories were often improvisational and included fairy tales, legends, puzzles, riddles, and stories. As the centuries passed, Hindu and Islamic stories were mixed in—including the two great Hindu epic stories, *Mahabharata* and the *Ramayana*—and writers sought to hone their craft using their own regional dialects. In the 1920s, Indonesian literature began to flourish alongside the independence movement. Authors began to experiment with the Bahasa Indonesia language.

The greatest of the modern Indonesian writers is Javanese novelist and short story writer Pramoedya Ananta Toer. First published in the late-1940s, Pramoedya's works have focused on Indonesian society both before and after independence. Some of his writings angered government officials, and he was arrested during the Suharto takeover in 1965 and imprisoned for more than fourteen years. Shortly after his release in 1979, Pramoedya began to publish his most famous work, a set of four historical novels known as the Buru Quartet, which explore Javanese society under Dutch colonial rule during the early 1900s. These highly acclaimed books have been translated into several different languages, including English.

During the Suharto years, Indonesia's news media was tightly controlled and rarely critical of the government. Since 1998, however, journalists have seized their new-found freedom, opening up the country to lively political debate.

Indonesians are avid television watchers, and most citizens who can afford them own satellite dishes. The government owns and controls Televisi Rupublik Indonesia (TVRI), which broadcasts news, movies, and other programming. Private stations broadcast similar programming,

THE YEAR OF LIVING DANGEROUSLY

Suharto's tumultuous rise to power was the backdrop for a popular film released in 1983, *The Year of Living Dangerously*. Based on a novel by Australian writer C. J. Koch, the film starred Mel Gibson. Gibson plays a reporter who finds himself swept up in the tide of political events in mid-1960s Indonesia.

including many films from the United States and India that have been dubbed or subtitled in Bahasa Indonesia.

To learn more about Indonesian literature, including author Pramoedya Ananta Toer, visit www.vgsbooks.com to find some links.

Sports and Recreation

Badminton, soccer, and volleyball are the most popular sports in Indonesia. The country has produced several world-class badminton players, including Susi Susanti and her husband, Allan Budi Kusuma, who each won gold medals in the sport at the 1992 Summer Olympic Games in Barcelona, Spain. At the 2000 Games in Sydney, Australia, Tony Gunawan and his partner Candra Wijaya also brought home gold for their home country in mixed doubles badminton. At the 2004 games, Taufik Hidayat brought home the gold in the men's singles event. Indonesians also scored two bronze medals.

Indonesians enjoy watching soccer as much as playing it. The game is particularly popular among the nation's youth, and both formal and informal soccer matches are held throughout the country year-round.

Among traditional Indonesian sports, the Madura bull races are the most famous. According to local tradition, the races originated between plowmen who competed for the entertainment of

Taufik Hidayat returns the birdie·in a badminton match against Bao Chunlai of China during the 2003 Indonesian Open tournament.

A contestant takes part in the grand finale **traditional bull race** of the year, also known as Karapan Sapi, in the Madurese city of Pamekasan.

Madurese kings. Over time, the sport has evolved into a lucrative industry and a popular form of entertainment. Trainers raise their bulls on a strict diet that includes honey, raw eggs, chili peppers, and beer. Races are held in stadiums year-round, culminating in an exciting grand finale in the island's capital of Pamekasan in October. In a thrilling and colorful spectacle, jockeys ride 100 yards (91 m) on a wooden sled, pulled by a pair of excited bulls.

Leisure activities in Indonesia include visits to the country's many beaches as well as trips to the countryside. On weekends Jakarta's main streets are closed to traffic and the city becomes a giant street party.

THE ECONOMY

As a country with a large population and an abundance of profitable natural resources such as oil and natural gas, Indonesia possesses the potential to be an economic powerhouse. Yet in the early 2000s, the country's economy is still struggling to develop and between one-quarter and one-half of the population lives in poverty. Indonesia's gross domestic product (GDP—the total amount of goods and services produced in one year) is about $760 billion. A recent comparison ranked Indonesia's economy as the fifteenth-largest in the world, just below South Korea's and just ahead of Australia's. But Indonesia's GDP per capita—the GDP divided by the population—is just $3,500, and ranks 149th in the world.

Under Suharto, economic development was a high priority. Beginning in the 1960s, the government set goals for the nation in the form of five-year plans, known by their Indonesian acronym of Repelita. The early Repelita focused on making the country's agricultural sector more productive and efficient and on improving infrastructure (such as

roads, highways, electricity grids). Later, Repelita focused on the trans-migration program and diversifying the economy.

On the whole, the programs were successful in meeting their goals and did much to help Indonesia develop economically. However, the country continued to face serious challenges in the form of widespread government corruption, a weak banking system, and a legal system that often fails to defend the rights of individual citizens. In mid-1997 many of the previous decades' gains were wiped out in a few short months by a severe drought and the Asian Financial Crisis. The latter, in particular, devastated the economy and left as much as half the population in severe poverty.

Since 1998 Indonesia's economy has struggled to recover from the crisis. Under Suharto's successors, the government has managed to stabilize the economy, but a series of disastrous events, including the 2002 terrorist attack on Bali and the 2004 tsunami, have made the country's full recovery more difficult.

Industry, Mining, and Energy

Industry accounts for 44 percent of Indonesia's GDP but employs just 16 percent of the workforce. Over the past several decades, the Indonesian government has worked to expand the manufacturing sector of its economy. As a result, industry surpassed agriculture as the top contributor to GDP in the early 1990s. Generally speaking, private companies produce the majority of Indonesia's consumer goods, such as food, beverages, tobacco products, textiles, clothing, and electrical appliances. Among these, a large number of small companies make handicrafts—batik and wood carvings, for example. The government owns and runs most of the larger, heavier industries, making chemicals, cement, glass, fertilizers, ceramics, machinery, and metal products.

The government also owns the nation's oil company, Pertamina. Pertamina extracts and refines Indonesia's petroleum. Most of the country's oil comes from Sumatra, Kalimantan, and from offshore wells in the Java and South China seas, as does much of its natural gas. Large processing plants on northern Sumatra and Kalimantan have helped to make Indonesia a leading exporter of liquefied natural gas. Most oil and gas exports go to Japan, South Korea, and Taiwan. Indonesia is a member of the international Organization of the Petroleum Exporting Countries (OPEC).

In addition to its large oil and gas reserves, Indonesia contains substantial deposits of tin and is a top world supplier of the metal. The nation's largest tin mines lie on the islands of Bangka and Belitung, off the southeastern coast of Sumatra.

OPEC

The Organization of the Petroleum Exporting Countries was established to coordinate its members' petroleum prices and output and to share technical and economic aid. OPEC was established in 1960 by five of the world's largest oil-producing countries—Saudi Arabia, Iran, Iraq, Kuwait, and Venezuela. Indonesia joined the organization in 1962. (Qatar, Libya, the United Arab Emirates, Algeria, and Nigeria make up the rest of the group.)

The organization's members own 80 percent of the world's proven oil reserves and account for 40 percent of the world's annual oil production. Critics have complained that OPEC is a cartel—an organization that works together to control prices—and that its policies keep oil prices higher than they would be if the countries competed with one another. Others have noted that OPEC's coordination of prices and output has provided stability to the oil market.

Men work at an **oil well** on Sumatra. Indonesia's oil industry has helped to fuel much of the country's economic development.

Miners have extracted considerable amounts of bauxite from Bintan Island. The mountains of Papua hold large reserves of copper, and workers take nickel from pits in Sulawesi. Indonesia also has deposits of gold, silver, sulfur, coal, and manganese.

Most of Indonesia's energy for electricity comes from oil, natural gas, and coal. Oil accounts for 47 percent of energy consumption, natural gas contributes 30 percent, and coal provides another 20 percent. The remaining 3 percent of Indonesia's energy needs are provided by hydroelectric, geothermal, wind, and solar power. For decades, the Indonesian government has subsidized gasoline and heating fuel in order to keep the price of these commodities low. In recent years, the government has attempted to save money by cutting these subsidies. But each of these attempts have been met with widespread protests.

To learn more about OPEC, visit www.vgsbooks.com to find a link to the organization's website.

⊙ Services, Tourism, and Trade

The service sector makes up the second-largest portion of Indonesia's economy, accounting for 40 percent of GDP and employing 39 percent of the workforce. The country's major service industries include government, education, health care, banking, transportation, and trade.

In recent years, an average of about 4 to 5 million tourists have visited Indonesia annually. The 2002 terrorist bombings on Bali had a significant impact on tourist visits the following year—causing a drop of about 500,000 visitors in 2003. The long-term effects of the 2004 tsunami disaster have yet to be determined.

Java, Bali, Sumatra, and Sulawesi offer foreigners a full range of accommodations, including hotels that are part of international chains. In other parts of the nation, special tourist facilities are lacking and visitors enter into the local way of life during their stay.

Bali is the most frequent destination for vacationers. The island's attractions include many colorful Hindu festivals, featuring music, dancing, ornate costumes, and highly decorated shrines. Bali, as well as Java and other islands, also draws visitors because of its natural beauty. Java contains the reconstructed Buddhist Temple of Borobudur, which dates from the eighth-century Sailendra dynasty. The remains of Prambanan—a tenth-century Hindu kingdom—bring tourists to the island too. Java also hosts many wayang performances.

The country's chief exports are oil and gas, electrical appliances, plywood, textiles, and rubber. Indonesia imports mainly machinery and equipment, chemicals, and food. The country's primary trading partners are Japan, Singapore, South Korea, China, the United States, Thailand, and Australia.

Agriculture, Forestry, and Fishing

About 45 percent of the Indonesian labor force works in agriculture. These workers produce about 16 percent of the country's GDP. Farmers cultivate approximately 6 percent of Indonesia's land.

Rice is the most widely grown crop. Most of the country's rice is grown on small family-owned plots of 2 to 3 acres (1 hectare). Farmers are able to grow two crops of rice per year in regions that have adequate water for irrigation. The Suharto government emphasized more rice production to make Indonesia self-sufficient in its staple food crop. In addition to sponsoring widespread irrigation systems, the programs have taught farmers the best and most efficient methods of growing crops. The government has also encouraged the use of fertilizers, pesticides, and higher-yielding seeds. Indonesia's transmigration program also tried to increase rice production by relocating farmers from overcrowded Java to farmland on less populated islands.

All of these measures were largely successful in increasing rice crop yields, and by the mid-1980s, Indonesia had reached its goal of self-sufficiency. However, since then the country has struggled to keep up with the demands of its growing population. In addition, pest infestations and a severe drought in 1997 have also had a negative effect on rice harvests. Other Indonesian food crops include coconuts, corn, peanuts, and sweet potatoes. Farmers also raise water buffalo as work animals and rear cattle, goats, and poultry for food.

Among cash crops, rubber is the most important. Indonesia also produces coffee, palm oil, sugarcane, tea, and tobacco. The majority of these cash crops are grown on large plantations. Most of these products are sold abroad.

Farmers on the larger islands often practice slash-and-burn agriculture. They cut trees and brush and then burn them to make clearings for their crops. Because farmers in these areas do not rotate their crops from year to year—for example, planting rice in a field one year and corn in it the next—their fields are soon worn out. Since worn-out fields require many years to regain soil nutrients, slash-and-burn agriculture is not productive over time.

Indonesia's forests and fishing grounds are among the largest in Asia. In recent decades, the government sought to conserve these resources so that timber harvests and fish catches will be plentiful in the future. Forests cover about 58 percent of the country, with most of this forested land lying on Kalimantan and in Papua. Although the state owns the forests, most licenses for timber cutting are issued to foreign companies. In past decades, failure to reforest has led to soil erosion and flooding of the harvested regions. In recent years, government forestry officials require all companies to plant seedlings in the regions that have been cut, although these laws have not always been enforced. Indonesia's drive to improve its forest management practices also stalled in the wake of the 1997 Asian Financial Crisis, as the government sought to revive the economy through increased production while ignoring many logging restrictions.

Loggers harvest much of the timber as roundwood (whole tree trunks), and they cut up teak, ebony, and other hardwoods into lumber. Other companies fashion rattan palm and bamboo into baskets, furniture, and housing material. Bark from mangrove trees is used to tan leather and make dyes. The cinchona tree's bark contains quinine, a medicine for the treatment of malaria.

TSUNAMI EFFECTS ON AGRICULTURE

The 2004 tsunami severely damaged the Sumatra coastline's cropland. About 89,000 to 123,500 acres (36,000 to 50,000 hectares) of land was affected by the waves. In addition to wiping out people, livestock, crops, and homes, the tidal waves also washed away topsoil and covered large areas with salt water. The high salt content has made much of the soil unusable.

Fishers on Bali gather onshore to pull their catch from nets. Using the small nets, the men set out in their traditional handmade boats several times per day.

In the Indonesian diet, fish are the main source of animal protein. The variety of fish in national waters includes tuna, sardines, scad, mackerel, and anchovies. Many commercial fishing companies operate in partnership with Japanese or other foreign enterprises. The most frequented fishing areas lie off the coasts of Sumatra and Papua. Traditional fishers in *prahu*—wooden boats with outriggers—catch most of the fish eaten within the country. The government protects the fishing grounds that these fishers use by not allowing large fishing companies into the area.

Transportation and Communications

Seas, swamps, mountains, and forests prevent Indonesians from traveling easily through the archipelago. The Dutch constructed road and rail networks on Java but did little to promote transportation links on the other islands. After World War II, even these roads and railways fell into disrepair, and independent Indonesia faced the challenge of improving its transportation system. Under Suharto, the government made transport infrastructure a high priority, spending a significant portion of the budget on roads, railways, and highways during the various five-year plans. Although these efforts greatly improved the country's road networks, they remained inadequate and many projects were abandoned in the wake of the 1997 Asian Financial Crisis.

Indonesia has 212,943 miles (342,700 km) of highway, with a little less than half of them paved. The majority—about 60 percent—are located on Java, Sumatra, and Bali. Roadways connect all major cities on these islands. Indonesia's 4,012 miles (6,458 km) of railroads run on Java, Madura, and Sumatra. Water transport (mainly rivers) remains the key source of transport on the other islands of the archipelago.

The Strait of Melaka, which separates Sumatra from Malaysia, is the world's busiest waterway. About one-quarter of the world's seaborne trade passes through the strait. It is 21 miles (34 km) wide and 560 miles long (900 km).

Buses, *bemos* (small vehicles), *becaks* (pedal-powered, open-air cabs), and bicycles move people through city streets and from village to village. The government runs a shipping company that connects the islands by sea. Private boats also ferry freight and passengers. Jakarta and Surabaya on Java and Medan on Sumatra are the nation's principal ports.

Garuda Indonesia is the government-sponsored international and domestic airline. Many private aircraft make short flights over the country's difficult terrain. International airports are located in Jakarta, Medan, and Denpasar (on Bali).

Becaks, also known as pedicabs, carry their passengers through a city street in Medan.

Indonesia's communications network has also been prey to the country's recent economic misfortunes. The country has about 7.8 million telephone landlines. But like many countries, mobile phones are becoming increasingly popular, with about 12 million phones in use. Indonesians enjoy watching television, and an estimated 14 million of them are in the country. Viewers have approximately 41 stations to choose from, many of them via satellite dishes. Internet use is growing rapidly among Indonesians—about 8 million people regularly use the Internet.

CORRUPTION

Corruption is widespread in Indonesia, and the country is often ranked one of the most corrupt in the world. Officials at all levels of government routinely embezzle public funds, while business owners must pay various bribes to government officials to start businesses, receive permits, and to escape harassment. These conditions have limited foreign investment, as many companies are reluctant to deal in such an environment.

Indonesia's legal system has not provided relief from corruption. In fact, judges are routinely bribed in exchange for favorable decisions. Since the vast majority of government officials are corrupt, they have little incentive to change the system. In recent years, activists have fought to reduce corruption in the country by attempting to bring offenders to justice, but their efforts have made little progress. Most Indonesians simply accept corruption as a way of life.

◉ The Future

Even before the 2004 tsunami disaster, Indonesia faced many challenges. President Yudhoyono won his position by promising to root out government corruption and improve the economy and the plight of the nation's poor. He also promised to seek peace between his government and the country's separatist groups. On corruption, Yudhoyono has received little cooperation from government officials.

His plans for improving the economy and the lives of the country's poor have been opposed as well. In 2005 Yudhoyono declared that the government would lower its subsidies on various fuels, including gasoline. The purpose of the cuts is to free up government money to fund other projects designed to help the economy. Previous presidents have proposed such cuts before but always backed down in the face of widespread protest. Yet Yudhoyono vowed to remain firm, and the subsidies were reduced on March 1, 2005.

Meanwhile, at least one positive result has come from the tsunami tragedy. In the wake of the terrible events, a desire for compromise arose between the government and the Acehnese separatists. Within weeks of the disaster, Indonesian government officials and Acehnese separatist leaders held talks in Finland aimed at ending the conflict. It is impossible to predict if these talks will lead to an end of the conflict. But the fact that the two sides are holding discussions is an encouraging sign for the future of Indonesia.

ca. 2000 B.C.   Malay people from the Southeast Asian mainland
begin migrating into the Indonesian archipelago.

CA. A.D. 200   Indonesians begin to exchange goods, such as cloves, timber,
and camphor, with Indian and Chinese traders. Travelers from
India and China spread their Hindu and Buddhist religions to the
archipelago's inhabitants.

CA. 600   Two large kingdoms—Mataram on Java and Srivijaya on Sumatra—
have emerged in the archipelago.

CA. 900   The Mataram kingdom constructs the giant Borobudur Buddhist Temple on
Java.

CA. 1200   The Buddhist-Hindu Singasari kingdom grows in size and influence in Indonesia.
Meanwhile, Muslim traders from the Middle East bring Islam to the archipelago.

1293   Singasari prince Vijaya founds the Majapahit kingdom.

1350   Hayam Wuruk ascends the throne of Majapahit, marking the beginning of the
golden age of Majapahit rule.

1400s   Islam spreads throughout the archipelago, with many Indonesians adopting the
religion.

1511   Portuguese explorer Afonso de Albuquerque conquers the kingdom of Melaka.

1596   Dutch ships enter the archipelago for the first time.

1610   The Dutch set up a trading center in Batavia.

1620s   Sultan Agung of the Mataram kingdom expands the boundaries of his realm to
include most of central Java.

1825   The Java War erupts between the Dutch and native Javanese leaders.

1830   The Java War ends with a Dutch victory. Dutch governor-general Joannes van
den Bosch introduces the Cultivation System. The system is highly profitable
for the Dutch but makes life very difficult for poor Indonesians.

1860   Dutch author Eduard Dekker publishes the novel *Max Havelaar*, exposing the
cruelty of the Cultivation System. The book sparks widespread outrage in
the Netherlands and changes in Dutch colonial policy.

1883   The Krakatau volcano erupts, creating the loudest explosion in
recorded history.

1908   A group of Indonesians found the Budi Utomo to speak out
against Dutch control of the archipelago.

1927   A young civil engineer, Sukarno, founds the Indonesian
Nationalist Party and calls for independence from the
Netherlands.

1939   World War II begins in Europe and Asia.

1942   Japanese forces defeat the Allies (including Britain, the
        Netherlands, and the United States) at the Battle of the Java Sea
        in February. Japanese forces occupy the archipelago.

1945   Sukarno outlines his principles of Pancasila on June 1. The Japanese surren-
        der to the Allies on August 15. Indonesian nationalists proclaim independence
        on August 17. Fighting erupts between Indonesian troops and the British troops
        stationed in Java.

1949   The Netherlands confirm Indonesia's independence by removing Dutch troops
        from the country.

1950   Indonesian nationalist leaders formally organize the Republic of Indonesia, with
        Sukarno as president.

1965   General Suharto halts an attempted coup d'état but begins to push Sukarno out of
        power.

1968   Suharto officially becomes president of Indonesia.

1970s   The Suharto government stresses economic development while responding violently to
        separatist movements in East Timor, Aceh, and Papua.

1980s   Suharto and his political party, Golkar, exercise nearly total control over Indonesian
        politics.

1997   The Asian Financial Crisis begins in Thailand and soon spreads to Indonesia, causing
        tremendous economic hardship.

1998   The bleak economic situation leads to riots in Jakarta. Suharto steps down in May. He
        is replaced by Vice President B. J. Habibie.

1999   In an August 30 referendum, East Timorese vote overwhelmingly for independence.
        Violence erupts in the area, prompting a UN peacekeeping force to enter East Timor.

2002   Terrorists set off two bombs on the island of Bali, killing more than two hundred
        people.

2004   The first direct presidential elections take place, making former army general
        Susilo Bambang Yudhoyono the country's new leader. A tremendous earthquake
        occurs off the coast of Sumatra, creating a massive tsunami that strikes the
        island's coast on December 26. At least 122,000 Indonesians die.

2005   As post-tsunami rescue efforts come to an end, leaders of the Acehnese
        separatist Free Aceh Movement begin talks with the Indonesian govern-
        ment in hopes of finding a solution to the Aceh conflict.

COUNTRY NAME Republic of Indonesia

AREA 705,192 square miles (1,826,440 sq. km) in land area

MAIN LANDFORMS Greater Sunda Islands (Java, Sulawesi, Sumatra, and Kalimantan); Lesser Sunda Islands (Bali, Lombok, Sumbawa, Flores, Sumba, Alor, and Timor); Maluku Islands (Halmahera, Ceram, Buru, and many other smaller islands); Papua; Borneo

HIGHEST POINT Puncak Jaya (Papua), 16,535 feet (5,040 m) above sea level

LOWEST POINT sea level

MAJOR RIVERS Asahan, Barito, Brantas, Digul, Hari, Kapuas, Mamberamo, Musi, Solo

CAPITAL CITY Jakarta

OTHER MAJOR CITIES Bandjarmasin, Makassar, Medan, Palembang, Surabaya

OFFICIAL LANGUAGE Bahasa Indonesia

MONETARY UNIT rupiah

CURRENCY

Indonesia's currency is the rupiah. The word roughly means "wrought silver" in the Indian Sanskrit language. The Indonesian government mints coins of 25, 50, 100, 500, and 1,000 rupiah. Notes are printed in denominations of 500, 1,000, 5,000, 10,000, 20,000, and 50,000, and 100,000 rupiah. Rupiah notes come in

a variety of colors, and their faces feature images of famous Indonesians. Backs of bills feature images of scenic locations.

The Indonesian flag was adopted on Independence Day, August 17, 1945. The flag's design is based on the banner of the old Majapahit kingdom. The red on top is said to symbolize the blood and sacrifice of the country's founders while the white is said to represent the human spirit.

The Indonesian national anthem is "Indonesia Raya" (Great Indonesia). The song was composed in 1928 by Wage Rudolf Supratman. The area that later became Indonesia was then ruled by the Dutch and lacked a national identity. The song encourages Indonesians to unite for the cause of a free and independent country.

Indonesia Raya (Great Indonesia)
Indonesia, my native land,
My place of birth,
Where I stand guard
Over my mother land.

Indonesia, my nationality,
My people and my country
Let us all cry
For united Indonesia.

Long live my land,
My nation and all my people
Arouse their spirit,
Arouse their bodies,
For Great Indonesia.

Great Indonesia, free and independent,
The land, the country I love
Great Indonesia, free and independent,
Long live Indonesia.

 Discover the melody of Indonesia's national anthem, "Indonesia Raya." Go to www.vgsbooks.com for a link.

RADEN AJENG KARTINI (1879–1904) This powerful advocate for woman's rights in Indonesia was born into a noble family in Jepara. Princess Kartini was one of the first Indonesian women to receive a Dutch education. She used her fluency in Dutch and her strong writing voice to bring attention to the plight of Indonesian women, who enjoyed few rights. Kartini explained her views in a series of letters to sympathetic Dutch activists, who passed them along to others. Kartini died at the age of twenty-five. Her letters were published a few years later and received worldwide attention. Her birthday, April 21, is a national holiday.

MEGAWATI SUKARNOPUTRI (b. 1947) Indonesia's president from 2001 to 2004 was born Dyah Permata Megawati Setiawati Sukarnoputri in Yogyakarta. She is the eldest daughter of Sukarno, Indonesia's first president. (Sukarnoputri means "daughter of Sukarno.") In the late 1990s, she became a symbol of the pro-democracy movement that pushed for the end of Suharto's rule. In the 1999 national elections, her new party, the Indonesian Democratic Party of Struggle, won the most votes, but Megawati was outmaneuvered for the presidency by her rival, Abdurrahman Wahid. Megawati became vice president and moved up to the top post when Wahid was impeached in 2001. She lost her bid for reelection in 2004 to Susilo Bambang Yudhoyono.

PRAMOEDYA ANANTA TOER (b. 1925) Indonesia's greatest novelist and short story writer was born in Blora, in central Java. Son of a schoolteacher, Pramoedya fought for independence from the Dutch following World War II. After being imprisoned by the Dutch in 1947, he wrote his first published novel, *Perburuan* (*The Fugitive*), in 1950. Following Indonesia's independence and his release from prison in 1949, Pramoedya published a stream of novels and short stories that earned him great attention. However, in 1965 he was imprisoned by the government and not released until 1980. But during his confinement, he wrote his most important works, the so-called Buru Quartet, which depicted Indonesian society under Dutch rule in the early twentieth century.

SUHARTO (b. 1921) Indonesia's second president was born in Kemusu Argamulja, on Java. He fought for Indonesia's independence and quickly rose through the ranks of the Indonesian military. In 1965 he thwarted a coup attempt and seized power from Sukarno. He was made acting president in 1967 and president in 1968. Under Suharto Indonesia experienced strong economic growth and made many strides in developing the country's infrastructure and industries. However, Suharto's rule was also characterized by government corruption, restrictions of political freedom, and violent crackdowns against separatist groups. The collapse of Indonesia's economy in the wake of the 1997 Asian Financial Crisis eventually led to Suharto's downfall in May 1998.

TOMMY SUHARTO (b. 1962) Hutomo Mandala Putra, known as Tommy

Suharto, is the son of Indonesia's second president. As a member of the Suharto family, Tommy used his influence to enrich himself by taking a cut of funds from various government and private business projects. By 2000 his financial worth was estimated at $800 million. In 1999 he was convicted of fraud and sentenced to eighteen months in jail. Tommy promptly escaped, and in a story that earned international headlines, he remained at large for a year. During this period, the judge who had convicted Tommy was murdered. After Tommy's capture in 2001, he was convicted of arranging the murder of the judge and is serving a fifteen-year prison sentence.

SUKARNO (1901–1970) Indonesia's first president was born in Surabaya. After earning a degree in civil engineering in 1927, he turned to politics and became a leading activist for Indonesian independence. On June 1, 1945, Sukarno outlined his concept of Pancasila in a famous speech. Weeks later, he declared Indonesia's independence and led the country in its successful struggle against Dutch rule. During his years as president, Sukarno was frequently criticized for lacking a coherent policy for the country's development. In 1965 he was pushed out of power by Suharto, although he remained president in name for a few more years.

SURABAYA SUE (1908–1997) One of Indonesia's most beloved freedom fighters, she was born Muriel Pearson in Scotland. Pearson traveled to Bali in her early twenties and soon fell in love with Indonesia. She resisted the Japanese occupation during World War II and was imprisoned and tortured by the Japanese for two years. After her release, she wrote about her ordeal in a famous autobiography, *Revolt in Paradise*. She later went on to join the Indonesian independence movement, for which she broadcast news reports from an underground radio station. In this latter role, she earned her famous nickname, Surabaya Sue.

SUSI SUSANTI (b. 1971) Indonesia's first gold-medal winner was born in Tasikmalaya (Java). Susanti began playing and competing in badminton at the age of eight and soon became a world-class player. At the 1992 Summer Olympic Games, Susanti dominated the competition in the early rounds before winning a spirited gold-medal match against her South Korean opponent. Susanti won the bronze medal at the 1996 Olympic Games in Atlanta.

SUSILO BAMBANG YUDHOYONO (b. 1949) Yudhoyono came to power in 2004 as the first directly elected president in Indonesian history. Born in East Java in 1973, he joined the army as an officer and served several tours of duty during the Indonesian invasion of East Timor. He left the military to become a government official in 2000. A year later, he gained the attention of the public when he was fired for refusing to back a plan to derail President Wahid's impeachment. Yudhoyono is seen as a person of integrity, and Indonesians have placed great hopes in his presidency.

BALI Home to beautiful sandy beaches and vibrant green forests, Bali is a favorite destination for tourists from around the world. Things to do there include snorkeling in the clear waters of the northern coast, soaking up sun on the island's countless beaches, hiking in the scenic Central Mountains, and experiencing Bali's fascinating Hindu culture and crafts.

BOROBUDUR Located in central Java, this breathtaking edifice is the largest Buddhist temple in the world and one of Indonesia's top tourist attractions. Built between A.D. 750 and 850, the massive Borobudur contains more than 2.1 million cubic feet (60,000 cubic m) of carved stone, including countless pieces of ornate sculpture.

JAKARTA Indonesia's capital is one of the world's largest cities and a fascinating melting pot of Indonesian culture. The city is populated not only by millions of Javanese but also by natives of the archipelago's far-flung islands. Top attractions include the Kota district, the former hub of Dutch colonial Indonesia and home to an interesting assortment of eighteenth- and nineteenth-century colonial homes.

KALIMANTAN Indonesia's portion of this island is a popular destination for adventurous tourists. The island is home to numerous national parks, featuring a wide array of unique plants and animals. Visitors can also catch a glimpse of the unique culture of the indigenous Dayak people and their traditional lifestyle.

THE MALUKUS The Spice Islands of colonial days are known for their friendly inhabitants and lush, uncrowded white sand beaches. The nearby Banda Islands offer clear waters for snorkeling, historic forts from Indonesian's colonial days, and tours of nutmeg plantations.

SULAWESI Like so many of Indonesia's islands, Sulawesi features warm, sandy beaches and many good sites for underwater exploration. The island's many national parks are home to a wealth of exotic wildlife, and the island's largest city, Makassar, is famous for its excellent seafood restaurants.

SUMATRA Known in ancient times as Swarnadwipa (Island of Gold) for its many abundant natural resources, Sumatra is filled with natural beauty and is home to a wide variety of ethnic groups. Attractions include scenic Danau (Lake) Toba, the largest lake in Southeast Asia, which is tucked into the misty mountains of a dormant volcano. The island's Bohorok Orangutan Viewing Center provides a unique opportunity to see these famous animals up close. The smaller islands that ring Sumatra are some of the best locations for undersea diving in the world. The island was a growing tourist haven before the 2004 tsunami disaster, and the Indonesian government hopes that a return of tourism will help Sumatra's revival.

animism: a religious practice of spirit worship. Spirit (conscious life) is believed to inhabit natural objects, natural events (such as storms and lightning), and human ancestors.

archipelago: a group of islands

batik: the Indonesian art of creating vivid colors and designs on fabric using dye and wax

Buddhism: a religion that was established by Siddhartha Gautama, known as the Buddha, in India in the sixth century B.C. Buddhism teaches that the way to enlightenment is through meditation and self-knowledge.

colony: a territory governed by a distant nation and inhabited in part by settlers from the governing nation

coup d'état: a sudden and decisive political action, with or without force, that usually results in a change of government

gross domestic product (GDP): a measure of the total value of goods and services produced within a country in a year. A similar measurement is gross national product (GNP). GDP and GNP are often measured in purchasing power parity (PPP). PPP converts values to international dollars, making it possible to compare how much similar goods and services cost to the residents of different countries.

Hinduism: a polytheistic religion (worshipping multiple gods) founded by Aryans who migrated to India in the fifth century B.C. Hinduism's sacred texts are called the Vedas, and Hindus believe that all living things are part of the divine.

infrastructure: the system of public works of a country, including roads, highways, railways, sewers, and telephone lines

monsoon: a seasonal wind that typically blows from the southwest and is usually accompanied by heavy rains

nationalists: people who follow the philosophy of nationalism, which values loyalty to one's own nation above all else. Nationalist goals may include preservation of national culture, fulfillment of the nation's needs, and the nation's independence from outside influence.

Pancasila: the Indonesian state philosophy as outlined by Sukarno, the country's first president. Pancasila is based on five interrelated principles: belief in one supreme God, just and civilized humanitarianism, the unity of Indonesia, popular rule as achieved through consultation among citizens, and social justice for all Indonesians.

prahu: wooden sailboats used by Indonesian fishers

referendum: a direct vote by the people to approve or reject a law or government measure

separatist: a person or group who seeks independence for a political unit

strait: a narrow waterway that connects two large bodies of water

tsunami: a tidal wave caused by an undersea earthquake or volcanic eruption

BBC (British Broadcasting Corporation) *News Online.* **2005.**
http://news.bbc.co.uk/2/hi/asia-pacific/default.stm (March 24, 2005).
The BBC's Asia-Pacific section is a helpful resource for news on Indonesia and other Asian and Pacific nations.

Brown, Colin. *A Short History of Indonesia: The Unlikely Nation?* **Crows Nest, New South Wales, AU: Allen and Unwin, 2003.**
Written by an Australian historian, this brief and readable book provides a clear overview of Indonesia's history, from prehistoric times to the twenty-first century.

Dorai, Francis, ed. *Insight Guide: Indonesia.* **5th ed. London: APA Publications, 2001.**
The Discovery Channel's series of Insight Guides focuses on the people and cultures of numerous exotic countries. The Indonesia volume is packed with stunning color photos and provides valuable insight on the country's varied peoples and cultures.

The Economist. **2005.**
http://www.economist.com (March 24, 2005).
Both the website and print edition of this British newspaper provide up-to-date coverage of Indonesian news and events.

Europa Publications. *Regional Surveys: The Far East and Australasia, 2004.* **London: Europa Publications, Ltd., 2003.**
Europa's regional surveys provide a wealth of valuable information about the history, economy, and population of countries around the world, including Indonesia.

Frederick, William H., and Robert L. Worden, eds. *Indonesia: A Country Study.* **5th ed. Washington, DC: Federal Research Division, Library of Congress, 1993.**
The Indonesia volume from the Library of Congress's Area Handbook series provides clear and objective information about Indonesia's history, geography, economy, society, and military.

Jordis, Christine. *Bali, Java, in My Dreams.* **London: The Harvill Press, 2002.**
In writing about her many visits to Indonesia, British writer Christine Jordis creates a vivid and colorful impression of two of Indonesia's most populous and culturally rich islands.

Population Reference Bureau. **2005.**
http://www.prb.org/ (March 24, 2005).
The annual statistics on this site provide a wealth of data on Indonesian population, birth and death rates, fertility rate, infant mortality rate, and other useful demographic information.

Ramage, Douglas. *Politics in Indonesia: Democracy, Islam, and the Ideology of Tolerance.* **New York: Routledge, 1995.**
This book, written by an expert on Indonesian affairs, is an in-depth study and analysis of Indonesia's political system during the later years of Suharto's rule.

Selected Bibliography

Sinjorgo, Michael. *Culture Shock! Succeed in Business: The Essential Guide for Business and Investment: Indonesia.* **Portland, OR: Graphic Arts Center Publishing Company, 1997.**
The Culture Shock series provides valuable insights on the cultures of many nations. This volume in the series focuses on culture in Indonesia from a businessperson's perspective.

Taylor, Jean Gelman. *Indonesia: Peoples and Histories.* **New Haven, CT: Yale University Press, 2003.**
Historian Jean Gelman Taylor weaves political events into this social history of Indonesia's varied and diverse ethnic groups.

Van Dijk, Kees. *A Country in Despair: Indonesia between 1997 and 2000.* **Leiden, NL: KITLV Press, 2002.**
This book, written by a Dutch historian, traces one of the most tumultuous eras in Indonesian history.

Asia-art.net
http://www.asia-art.net/batik.html
Learn more about batik, the Indonesian craft of turning fabric into beautiful art, from this website.

BBC Country Profile: Indonesia
http://news.bbc.co.uk/2/hi/asia-pacific/country_profiles/1260544.stm
Learn about Indonesia's current political situation from this BBC News Web page. It includes a brief history of the country, profiles of Indonesia's leaders, and background information on the country's media.

Central Intelligence Agency (CIA)
http://www.cia.gov/cia/publications/factbook/geos/id.html
The "World Factbook" section of the CIA's website contains basic information on Indonesia's geography, people, economy, government, communications, transportation, military, and transnational issues.

CNN.com In-Depth Specials: Kalimantan's Agony: The Failure of Transmigrasi
http://www.cnn.com/SPECIALS/2001/kalimantan/
This feature from the Cable News Network's website contains news reports and analysis about the Indonesian government's largely unsuccessful transmigration campaign.

Cornell, Kari, and Merry Anwar. *Cooking the Indonesian Way.* **Minneapolis: Lerner Publications Company, 2004.**
Learn more about Indonesia's unique cuisine from this volume from Lerner's Easy Menu Ethnic Cookbooks series.

Embassy of Indonesia, Washington, D.C.
http://www.embassyofindonesia.org/
The website of the Republic of Indonesia Embassy in Washington, D.C., features a variety of useful information about the country.

The Jakarta Post.com
http://www.thejakartapost.com/headlines.asp
The online edition of the largest English newspaper in Indonesia features local, national, and business news, as well as sports and much more.

Kartini, Raden Ajeng. *Letters of a Javanese Princess.* **Lanham, MD: University Press of America, 1992.**
This book is a recent English translation of the famous letters of Indonesia's woman's rights pioneer Raden Ajeng Kartini.

McGuinn, Taro. *East Timor: Island in Turmoil.* **Minneapolis: Lerner Publications Company, 1998.**
Learn more about the long and bloody East Timor conflict from this volume in Lerner's World in Conflict series.

Mirpuri, Gori, and Robert Cooper. *Indonesia.* **2nd ed. New York: Benchmark Books, 2002.**
This volume in the Cultures of the World series provides an overview of Indonesia's geography, history, government, economy, environment, people, and culture.

Pramoedya Ananta Toer. *This Earth of Mankind.* **New York: Penguin Books Inc., 1996.**

This book is the first volume in Pramoedya Ananta Toer's famous Buru Quartet series. Written during Pramoedya's confinement in Indonesia's Buru Island prison colony, the story follows the early adulthood of a young student, Minke, living in Indonesia during the early twentieth century.

————. *Child of All Nations.* **New York: Penguin Books, Inc., 1996.**

The second volume of Pramoedya's Buru Quartet follows the next stage of Minke's life as he struggles with racism and class conflicts in early twentieth-century Indonesia.

Souza, D. M. *Powerful Waves.* **Minneapolis: Carolrhoda Books, Inc., 1992.**

Learn more about tsunamis and other powerful waves from this book in Carolrhoda's Nature in Action series.

vgsbooks.com
http://www.vgsbooks.com

Visit www.vgsbooks.com, the home page of the Visual Geography Series®. You can get linked to all sorts of useful online information, including geographical, historical, demographic, cultural, and economic websites. The www.vgs-books.com site is a great resource for late-breaking news and statistics.

Witten, Patrick, et al. *Indonesia.* **7th ed. Oakland: Lonely Planet Publications, 2003.**

This volume in the Lonely Planet Travel Guides is a valuable resource on the geography, history, culture, people, and economy of Indonesia.

Captions for photos appearing on cover and chapter openers:

Cover: Rice terraces in Bali. Rice is an important part of Indonesia's history. In the eighth century, some kings levied taxes in rice rather than currency. The growing importance of rice cultivation over the last fifteen hundred years has transformed Indonesia's dense, forested landscape into fields and settlements.

pp. 4–5 The devastation of the tsunami in 2004 was most acutely felt in Banda Aceh on Sumatra. This village near the coast was almost entirely wiped out.

pp. 8–9 The Pura Ulun Danu temple, dedicated to Dewi Danu, goddess of the waters, sits on Lake Bratan in Bali. This Hindu and Buddhist temple dates from the seventeenth century A.D.

pp. 20–21 In this drawing, the leader of Java meets with a Dutch naval officer to negotiate a trade agreement.

pp. 36–37 Muslim students study in their classroom at Al-Islam boarding school in Tenggulun, East Java.

pp. 44–45 *Wayang golek* puppets in Central Java. There are three types of wayang puppets. The traditional wayang puppets are the *wayang kulit*, which are leather figures used to tell Hindu-Buddhist myths and folktales, such as the *Mahabharata* and *Ramayana*. Wayang golek puppets are three-dimensional wooden puppets that usually tell the same stories as the wayang kulit, but they also have their own set of tales inspired by Islamic myths. *Wayang klitik* are flat, wooden puppets used primarily in East Java and are associated with Damar Wulan stories that tell of a handsome prince who became ruler of the Majapahit kingdom.

pp. 56–57 A farmer plows his rice field with the aid of water buffalo. When harnessed to a plow, the water buffalo's strength helps break up mud clods in the field. Water buffalo are valued for more than just their strength. Their manure is used as fertilizer for the fields.